AF335447

A DESCRIPTIVE CATALOGUE *of the* JORGE LUIS BORGES COLLECTION *at the* UNIVERSITY OF VIRGINIA LIBRARY

A DESCRIPTIVE CATALOGUE *of the* JORGE LUIS BORGES COLLECTION *at the* UNIVERSITY OF VIRGINIA LIBRARY

C. Jared Loewenstein

University Press of Virginia
Charlottesville and London

THE UNIVERSITY PRESS OF VIRGINIA

First published 1993

Library of Congress Cataloging-in-Publication Data

Loewenstein, C. Jared.
A descriptive catalogue of the Jorge Luis Borges collection at the University of Virginia Library / by C. Jared Loewenstein.
p. cm.
Includes bibliographical references (p.) and indexes.
ISBN 0-8139-1333-0 (cloth)
1. Borges, Jorge Luis, 1899- --Bibliography--Catalogs.
2. University of Virginia. Library--Catalogs. I. University of Virginia. Library. II. Title.
Z8109.36.L63 1991
[PQ7797.B635]
016.868--dc20 91-35120
CIP

Printed in the United States of America

IN MEMORY OF

my parents

ELIZABETH KEYES LOEWENSTEIN

PAUL LUDWIG LOEWENSTEIN

and my aunt

MARY GERTRUDE KEYES

CONTENTS

FOREWORD

Normally, when an author dies, there is a flurry of critical and editorial activity, followed by a phase of declining interest until his or her work undergoes a reevaluation. This has not been the case with Borges, whose death in June 1986 hardly produced a ripple in the stream of publications dealing with his life and work. It rose to a flood in the 1980s and shows no sign of abating. Even by 1973, when Becco's *Jorge Luis Borges, bibliografía total 1923-1973* appeared, the number of entries exceeded thirteen hundred. One trembles to think what the number must have risen to since then.

It is noteworthy that much of what has come out has been essentially concerned with interpretation, that is to say, with content and thematics. Nor is this in any way invalid. Borges, despite his immense, worldwide popularity, is a difficult writer, and whatever contributes to improving the dialogue between his work and its readers is welcome. But preoccupation with Borges' thought and with the meaning of what he has written, whether in general or in relation to specific works, has tended to overshadow critical attempts to come to terms with the techniques and strategies he employed, that is to say, with the genuinely "writerly" aspect of his work. Inspection of recent issues of *The Modern Language Association of America Annual Bibliography* or *The Year's Work in Modern Language Studies* quickly reveals the utter disproportion that exists between the effort expended on discussing what Borges has said in this or that area of his work and the time devoted to critical analysis of the way he has said it. There can be no real doubt that one of the best ways forward in Borges studies is toward close examination of the functionality of the structures and devices he uses in his prose and the careful examination of the patterns and language of his poetry.

But in order to be able to bring close textual analysis to bear on Borges, we need reliable information about the origins and development of the texts themselves, and the lack of this is a serious obstacle. A start was made recently by Tommaso Scarano in his valuable *Varianti a stampa nella poesia del primo Borges* (Pisa: Giardini, 1987). To all but the most devoted students of Borges' early poetry this unpretentious but painstaking book came as a revelation. How many of us were really aware that what we read in the latest edition of Borges' first three volumes of poetry represents only about 1,200 of the original almost 2,000 lines? Of the lines that survive, moreover, almost half have been substantially altered. Study of the variants Scarano has recorded gives us one of the keys to Borges' poetic evolution, because some of the alterations were made twenty and even thirty years later than the date of the original publications.

Yet Scarano was considering only three works. How much more valuable must be similar information waiting to be collected about the rest of Borges' production as well as the clues contained in the tiny amount of manuscript sources that escaped destruction by Borges himself. The University of Virginia Library has brought together under one roof by far the best existing collection of Borges' early editions, contributions to periodicals and other publications, and a majority of the available manuscripts. No serious textual, as distinct from critical, work on Borges on any scale will henceforth be possible without consultation of this collection. In the period in which C. Jared Loewenstein has been working on its acquisition and cataloguing, it has grown so rapidly that what was originally envisaged as a small task has turned over the years into a complex undertaking exciting to all Borges scholars and indeed to all students of modern Argentine literature.

This is not to say that in the Virginia Borges Collection we shall discover a "lost" Borges, different from the author we know. What we chiefly discover is ample confirmation that the various complete works not only differ among themselves in inclusiveness but are far less complete than we already knew them to be. In one sense this is no surprise. It is notorious that Borges persistently refused to republish *Inquisiciones* and *El tamaño de mi esperanza* after the first editions and *El idioma de los argentinos* after the second. Nor does he seem to have collected the historically important essays on *ultraísmo* that appeared in *Nosotros* and *Prisma* in November and December 1921. It is pleasing to know that they can all be examined together in this collection, which contains sets of *Proa, Prisma, Los anales de Buenos Aires*, and *Martín Fierro*. These form the first category of items that are of overwhelming interest to every Borges scholar. When we set beside them the three issues of *Destiempo* (1936) (all that appeared) and the sets of *La vida literaria* (1932) and *Poesía* (1933), we begin to appreciate the extent of the collection's wealth.

Turning to Borges' own creative work, we notice under the heading "Poetry" a number of apparently uncollected pieces and some others belonging to "Museo" that do not seem to have found their way into *El hacedor*. It is not clear why these items were excluded from the canon or whether "Salmos," for example, has anything to do with the lost "Salmo" mentioned by Carlos Meneses in his *Poesía juvenil de Jorge Luis Borges*. Provisionally they may be added to those identified and republished by Meneses in the booklet just mentioned and those exhumed by Linda Maier in *Modern Language Notes,* 102, 1987. In general, however, what is interesting are the first editions of the earliest works and the original location and texts of individual poems included in later collections. When the time comes for a proper critical edition of Borges' poetry to be prepared, with the various texts collated, the material gathered here will be indispensable. Meanwhile, it is good to be able to see at a glance from this catalogue the date and place of first publication of a good number of important poems. It is to be hoped that, at the very least, the existence of this collection will lead to reprinting of the early first editions of Borges' verse.

It is a different story with the essays by Borges held in the collection. A glance at this section of the catalogue reveals how many of his contributions to *Nosotros, Síntesis, Los anales de Buenos Aires, Clarín, Cuadernos, Testigo, Europa,* and even to journals such as *La revista de la Universidad de Buenos Aires* and *La torre*, to say nothing of *Proa* and most of all *Sur*, are not in any of the complete works. Topics include: Alfonso Reyes, Cervantes, Supervielle, Nabokov, Tagore, Francisco Ayala, Wells, Juan Ramón Jiménez, Joyce, Lugones, Apollinaire, Lawrence, detective fiction, *ultraísmo*, Shakespeare, Pirandello, Kafka, Swinburne, Whitman, and Güiraldes. It is a list to make one gasp. Nor are these pieces by any means all minor, if indeed we can ever speak of minor writings by a figure like Borges. As this foreword was being written a useful piece on one of these uncollected items (Essays, no. 146) was published in France by Monique Joly. Many others will now surely follow. In this connection, too, one must mention numerous prefaces Borges has written at different times that do not appear in his collected *Prólogos*. Some of them are virtually unknown. They are a treasure indeed, as are his translations which, especially in the case of those of Faulkner and Whitman, deserve closer study.

The section of the catalogue on the short stories contains fewer surprises. I have counted only three uncollected items. But once more there are invaluable first editions and copies of the originally published texts of individual tales that were later gathered into books. Only with this material to hand is it possible to guarantee the eventual publication of completely reliable texts.

Special mention, of course, must be made of the manuscripts. It is doubtful, because of their extreme scarcity, whether more than a few will ever come together in one place. The nineteen examples mentioned here are the gems of the Virginia Borges Collection, including as they do the first draft of the unforgettable "Sentirse en la muerte" and autographs of "La casa de Asterión" and "El muerto" (from *El aleph*), with corrections and variants. This is the first catalogue of the holdings of Borges' work and related items by an individual institution so far published. It makes a very special contribution to Borges studies. As has been mentioned, nothing like the full corpus of Borges' work will be readily available to scholars and students for many years to come, and even then some texts may not be fully reliable until much painstaking work has been carried out. The process is only just beginning. With the appearance of this catalogue much of the ground has been cleared. It is a landmark. For the first time we know where the principal hoard of materials is to be found and exactly what it contains. It marks the first step to putting textual studies of Borges' work on a firm foundation and provides fresh incentives for carrying them out. Those who have been working on Borges for years can only envy newcomers to the field for whom this catalogue will be an indispensable tool.

Donald L. Shaw
Brown-Forman Professor of Spanish American Literature
Chairman, Department of Spanish, Italian, and Portuguese
University of Virginia

INTRODUCTION

The Jorge Luis Borges Collection at the University of Virginia Library had its genesis in a telephone call I received at home one Sunday evening in February 1977; it was from an antiquarian bookseller in Latin America. We had met some time earlier at an international conference of librarians, and the bookseller thus knew of the Library's strong interest in contemporary Latin American literature. He called to offer for sale a collection of approximately 400 titles on Borges, both original works--particularly early first editions--and a large body of Borges criticism. A number of these titles had been collected originally by a friend of Borges, a fellow poet from the 1920s. Many of the original works bore inscriptions by their celebrated author; there was an unpublished manuscript poem intended for Borges' first book, *Fervor de Buenos Aires* (1923), and many other treasures in the group of materials for sale. I spent a sleepless night following that telephone conversation; the next day I secured the approval of the University Librarian for the necessary expenditure to obtain the entire collection.

Thus began an acquisitions project that would eventually yield the results described within these pages, one that has attracted Borges scholars from near and far to Charlottesville over the past thirteen years. Nevertheless, until a catalogue of these materials could be prepared (a task requiring far more time and energy than I had originally anticipated), much of what was known about them was received by word of mouth among interested researchers, since the Library did not then have the resources at its disposal to catalogue fully the enormous number of Borges titles.

This descriptive catalogue of the Borges Collection at the University of Virginia Library is intended to serve several purposes. It details bibliographically the contents of the Library's holdings of material by and about Borges, which are by a significant margin the most complete in existence. Borges' international reputation as a man of letters is, of course, obvious; his works, however, have often been so altered in printings subsequent to their first appearance that the original versions in many cases may bear little resemblance to later ones. Since the great majority of Borges' early (1921-1944) publications exist in only a small handful of surviving copies, the Virginia collection is especially impressive, including as it does virtually all first editions of these titles. Also to be found here are nearly all original literary manuscripts--published and unpublished--that have appeared for sale during the past decade, as well as a number of unpublished originals of letters written by Borges. The following pages also describe copies of all Borges' later works, together with variant printings, editions, and translations. Borges' contributions to numerous anthologies, his collaborative writings, prologues, and translations or editions by Borges of the works of other writers also appear in this catalogue, as do extensive listings of critical or biographical material pertaining to Borges. Other items of interest include a significant collection of unpublished correspondence between Ben Belitt and Norman Thomas di Giovanni concerning the translation of Borges' poetry into English, a selection of interviews with the author, and a list of bibliographical titles. Entries are indexed by author (except for those by Borges himself) and by title (including Borges' works). The whole is preceded by an enlightening essay by one of the most distinguished scholars in the world of Borges studies, Donald L. Shaw, presently at the University of Virginia.

The catalogue that follows, therefore, is also a literary guide to the development and transmission of many of Borges' texts from initial manuscript or earliest printed versions through later editions and translations, outlining a journey that may be taken only by means of the material described herein. The Virginia collection is thus doubly significant in that researchers can not only read Borges' earliest works in the scarce original versions, but they can also trace the changes in his writings from the beginnings of his career until his last publication. Since Borges often sought to suppress his "youthful" work by either destroying, refusing to reprint, or rewriting many pieces, scholars will be able to discover many new aspects of the author's production and to explore his writings from all perspectives--biographical, sociohistorical, philosophical, stylistic, formalistic--by following specific texts through all versions. In part, an unknown Borges emerges here.

Before discussing certain details pertaining to the bibliographic text of the catalogue, several additional general statements should be made. This listing of Borges materials is not intended as the definitive descriptive bibliography in this field; as the book's title indicates, this is a catalogue, with annotations, of a specific collection of items. It is, moreover, different from other Borges bibliographies in several respects. First, and most obviously, it contains a good deal of material not cited elsewhere; the manuscripts, many variants, some of the miscellany, and many of Borges' contributions to journals found here are excellent examples of that fact. Furthermore, the compiler had the advantage of working directly with the materials themselves, thereby making it possible to include such details as full pagination statements for all items cited. It must also be pointed out that the collection described does not include any Borges titles held by the Library outside those found in its Special Collections Department; there are thus a few works held in the Library's general collections that are not represented here. Finally, ordinary materials received since final preparation of this catalogue was begun in 1986 are also not included.

The bibliographical entries in this catalogue are organized in what is intended as a logical system: original works by Borges are cited first, divided into categories by genre (not an insignificant task in itself, since Borges' writing often resists such generic classifications); followed by listings of original manuscript materials; various types of miscellaneous items relating to Borges that defy placement elsewhere; a large section on literary criticism and biographies of the author; other bibliographies of Borges titles; and author-title indexes. Because this is a catalogue rather than a true bibliography in the strictest sense of the term, citations are arranged on an alphabetical basis (initial articles being ignored for filing purposes) within each section; such an arrangement does not, therefore, take into account the chronology of later editions.

Each bibliographic entry includes: author (primary author in cases of collaboration); full title; edition; imprint statement (place of publication, publisher, and date); full pagination statement; size / format; and series statement. Additionally, a large number of citations, particularly for Borges' original works, are fully annotated with such data as: full edition / printing statement; provenance / association; transcription of the author's inscriptions where present; and analysis of contents. Entries are also referenced individually to Horacio Jorge Becco's *Jorge Luis Borges, bibliografía total 1923-1973,* published in 1973 in Argentina.

The specific format of the citations in this catalogue requires only brief comment. In the bibliographical portion of each, elements within square brackets are data inferred from a source other than the title page of the work cited. In the pagination statement, bracketed numbers refer to pages that do not themselves carry folios. Spine height, given in centimeters, includes binding unless otherwise stated in an annotation. The Becco reference numbers found in appropriate item listings are bracketed where the titles in the Virginia collection are variants of those cited by Becco. Apparent discrepancies in citation format may be accounted for by the fact that each entry is intended to represent an exact transcription of a specific title page.

It should be added that, while the compiler has been assisted by many individuals while engaged in the present work (their names appear below), he is solely responsible for any errors that must inevitably arise in such a book. It is to be hoped that those mistakes will not seriously hamper its research value to Borges scholars and others, whose tolerance is sincerely appreciated.

No endeavor of the kind typified by the present volume can be the work of a single individual. It has necessarily involved the cooperation and assistance of many people over a very considerable period of time. I wish to express my sincere appreciation to the persons and institutions who contributed so unstintingly to the preparation of this catalogue, despite the certainty that my fallible memory will omit those to whom I apologize in advance.

First, to Sr. Dn. Alfredo Breitfeld; to University Librarian Ray W. Frantz, Jr., at the University of Virginia; to the entire staff, past and present, of the Library's Special Collections Department; and to Susan L. Foard, John M. McGuigan, and Gerald L. Trett, editors at the University Press of Virginia; my heartfelt thanks for their invaluable support. Professors David T. Haberly and Alfred J. Mac Adam of the University of Virginia's Department of Spanish, Italian, and Portuguese ably planned that department's co-sponsorship with the Library in October 1978 of a major Borges symposium that stimulated early public interest in the collection as it existed at that time. The National Endowment for the Humanities generously provided a grant that assisted in defraying the costs of publishing this catalogue. Professor Donald L. Shaw, who wrote the foreword, was a constant mentor and friend during the later phases of my research; he also offered numerous suggestions that made the final product a much better one than it could otherwise have been.

Very special thanks are reserved for my assistants in the Library who labored long and arduously on my behalf in the preparation of this work: to Karen Y. Carter, Suzanne H. Freeman, Linda S. Maier, and Margarita J. Wuellner; my sincerest expressions of warmth and appreciation. To my long-suffering and ever-patient Director for Collection Development, Kenneth O. Jensen; and to my talented colleague, North Europe Bibliographer James M. Campbell; my deepest gratitude for the many services they rendered.

To a small group of individuals whose participation in this project far exceeded all my expectations, I can only attempt, inadequately, to acknowledge my greatest debt and to offer my highest praise: to Silvia F. Erskine, who laboriously transcribed the original citations from my dictation; to Linda Phillips, who painstakingly prepared the very complicated final manuscript; to Sarah M. Drenan, who kept me unswervingly on track as the work neared completion; and to my wife, Jacqueline A. Rice, for her unflagging devotion during all the chaos this book created in our life.

Finally, to the late Jorge Luis Borges himself, whom I first met in 1968 and who, many years later, understood and at least tacitly approved "the labors of a fellow-librarian," as he once put it; my sincerest admiration and thanks. Although he will never hold this volume in his hands, I like to believe that it still carries his blessing.

C. Jared Loewenstein
Ibero-American Bibliographer
University of Virginia Library

A DESCRIPTIVE CATALOGUE
OF THE
JORGE LUIS BORGES COLLECTION
AT THE
UNIVERSITY OF VIRGINIA LIBRARY

I. WORKS (COLLECTED AND SELECTED)

1. Borges, Jorge Luis.

   "Anthology." (In: *Tri Quarterly*, no. 25, pp. [172]-221. Evanston, Ill., Fall 1972).

   Collection of poems and prose pieces by Borges translated into English, primarily by Norman Thomas di Giovanni.

2. Borges, Jorge Luis.

   Antología personal. Buenos Aires: Sur, [1961].
   [1-9] 10-193 [194-200] p. 19 cm.

   First edition.

   BECCO 78

3. Borges, Jorge Luis.

   Antología personal. Buenos Aires: Sur, [1964, c. 1961].
   [1-7] 8-185 [186-192]. 19 cm.

   Variant of first edition.

   [BECCO 78]

4. Borges, Jorge Luis.

   Antologia personale. Presentazione di Alberto Arbasino. Traduzione di Maria Vasta Dazzi. Milano: Longanesi & C., [1981].
   [i-v] vi-xviii, [1-3] 4-216 [217-218] p. 21 cm. (La gaja scienza, 36.)

   Italian translation of: *Antología personal.*

5. Borges, Jorge Luis.

L'artefice. A cura di Francesco Tentori Montalto. Milano: Rizzoli, 1982.
[1-4] 5-110 [111-120] p. 22.5 cm.
(La scala: il catalogo.)

Italian translation of: *El hacedor*.

6. Borges, Jorge Luis.

L'auteur et autres textes. El hacedor. Edition bilingue traduit de l'espagnol par Roger Caillois. [Paris:] Gallimard, [1971, c. 1965].
[1-7] 8-275 [276-280] p. 20.5 cm.
(Du monde entier.)

French translation of: *El hacedor*. Includes other selections translated from *Antología personal*.

BECCO 254

7. Borges, Jorge Luis.

L'auteur et autres textes. El hacedor. Edition bilingue. Traduit de l'espagnol par Roger Caillois. [Paris:] Gallimard, [1979, c. 1965].
[1-7] 8-275 [276-280] p. 20.5 cm.
(Du monde entier.)

[BECCO 254]

8. Borges, Jorge Luis.

Borges, a Reader. A Selection from the Writings of Jorge Luis Borges. Edited by Emir Rodríguez Monegal and Alastair Reid. New York: E. P. Dutton, [1981].
[i-iv] v-xi [xii], [1-2] 3-369 [370-372] p. 24 cm.

First edition.

9. Borges, Jorge Luis.

Borges--fra A til Z. Oversatt fra Spansk av Kjell Risvik. Oslo: Gyldendal Norsk Forlag, [1979].
[i-iv], [1-6] 7-214 [215-220] p. 19 cm.
(Lanterne-bøkene, 447.)

Norwegian translations of: *El aleph, Otras inquisiciones, El hacedor, El informe de Brodie.*

10. Borges, Jorge Luis.

Borges über Borges. Autobiographischer Essay. Seminar über Fiction. Seminar über Dichtung. Epilog. Aus dem Englischen übersetzt von Christiane Meyer-Clason. [München:] Carl Hanser Verlag, [1980].
[1-6] 7-144 [145-148] p. 19 cm.
(Gesammelte Werke, 9.)

German translations of English and Spanish originals.

11. Borges, Jorge Luis.

Borges und Ich. Gedichte und Prosa. [München:] Deutscher Taschenbuch Verlag, [1969].
[1-8] 9-139 [140-144] p. 18 cm.
(Sonderreihe, 69.)

German translation of: *El hacedor.* Gift of James M. Campbell.

[BECCO 239]

12. Borges, Jorge Luis.

Borges und Ich. Nach der Übersetzung von Karl August Horst, bearbeitet von Gisbert Haefs. Nachwort von Claudio Magris. [München:] Carl Hanser Verlag, [1982].
[1-6] 7-160 [161-164] p. 19 cm.
(Gesammelte Werke, 6.)

German translation of: *El hacedor*.

[BECCO 239]

13. Borges, Jorge Luis.

Diccionario privado de Jorge Luis Borges.
Recopilado y ordenado por Blas Matamoro.
[Madrid:] Altalena, [1979].
[1-8] 9-92 [93-96] p. 21 cm.
(Mundo ancho y propio.)

First edition.

14. Borges, Jorge Luis.

Dreamtigers. Translated from *El hacedor* (*The Maker*) by Mildred Boyer and Harold Morland. Introduction by Miguel Enguídanos. Woodcuts by Antonio Frasconi. Austin/London: University of Texas Press, [1978, c. 1964].
[1-8] 9-95 [96]. 22.5 cm.
(The Texas Pan American series.)

Fourth printing. Gift of C. Jared Loewenstein.

[BECCO 270]

15. Borges, Jorge Luis.

Erzählungen, 1935-1944. Nach der Übersetzung von Karl August Horst, bearbeitet von Gisbert Haefs. Nachwort von Lars Gustafsson. [München:] Carl Hanser Verlag, [1981].
[1-6] 7-255 [256] p. 19 cm.
(Gesammelte Werke, 3/I.)

German translation of: Obras completas.

16. Borges, Jorge Luis.

Erzählungen, 1975-1977. Übersetzung von Dieter E. Zimmer. Nachwort von Horst Bienek. [München:]

Carl Hanser Verlag, [1982].
[1-8] 9-143 [144] p. 19 cm.
(Gesammelte Werke, 4.)

German translation of: *Obras completas.*

17. Borges, Jorge Luis.

O fazedor. Tradução de Miguel Tamen. Revista por Luísa Costa Gomes e Juan Carlos Vásquez. [Lisboa:] Difusão Editorial, Lda., [1984].
[1-6] 7-137 [138-144] p. 23 cm.

Portuguese translation of: *El hacedor.*

18. Borges, Jorge Luis.

El hacedor. [Buenos Aires:] Emecé Editores, S.A., [1960].
[1-6] 7-109 [110-116] p. 18.5 cm.
(Obras completas, 9.)

First edition. 2 copies.

BECCO 13

19. Borges, Jorge Luis.

El hacedor. [Buenos Aires:] Emecé Editores, [1967, c. 1960].
[1-6] 7-113 [114-120] p. 19 cm.
(Obras completas, 9.)

Fourth printing.

[BECCO 77]

20. Borges, Jorge Luis.

El hacedor. Buenos Aires-Barcelona: Emecé Editores, [1967].
[1-6] 7-158 [159-164] p. 17 cm.

(Colección piragua, 131.)

Fifth edition.

[BECCO 77]

21. Borges, Jorge Luis.

Nova antologia pessoal. Tradução de Maria da Piedade M. Ferreira. [Lisboa:] Difusão Editorial, Lda., [1983].
[1-6] 7-238 [239-240] p. 22.5 cm.

Portuguese translation of: *Nueva antología personal.*

22. Borges, Jorge Luis.

Nueva antología personal. [Buenos Aires:] Emecé Editores, [1968].
[1-8] 9-305 [306-312] p. 20 cm.

BECCO 80

23. Borges, Jorge Luis.

Nuova antologia personale. Traduzione di Livio Bacchi Wilcock. [Milano:] Rizzoli Editore, [1976].
[1-6] 7-267 [268-272] p. 22.5 cm.
(La scala.)

Italian translation of: *Nueva antología personal.*

24. Borges, Jorge Luis.

Obras completas, 1923-1972. Buenos Aires: Emecé Editores, [1977, c. 1974].
[1-8] 9-1161 [1162-1168] p. 22 cm.

Eighth printing. Includes frontispiece portrait of Borges on unnumbered leaf.

25. Borges, Jorge Luis.

Obras completas, 1923-1972. Buenos Aires: Emecé Editores, [1978, c. 1974].
[1-8] 9-1161 [1162-1168] p. 22 cm.

Ninth printing. Includes frontispiece portrait of Borges on unnumbered leaf.

26. Borges, Jorge Luis.

Páginas de Jorge Luis Borges seleccionadas por el autor. Estudio preliminar de Alicia Jurado. Buenos Aires: Editorial Celtia, [1982].
[1-8] 9-269 [270-272] p. 21.5 cm.
(Colección escritores argentinos de hoy.)

First edition.

27. Borges, Jorge Luis.

A Personal Anthology. Edited and with a foreword by Anthony Kerrigan. New York: Grove Press, [1967].
[i-iv] v-x [xi-xii], 1-210 [211-212] p. 21 cm.

English translation of: *Antología personal.* Clothbound. 2 copies, one the gift of Joan St. C. Crane.

BECCO 275

28. Borges, Jorge Luis.

A Personal Anthology. Edited and with a foreword by Anthony Kerrigan. New York: Grove Press, Inc., [1967].
[1 unnumbered leaf], [i-iv] v-x [xi-xii], 1-210 p. 20.5 cm.

English translation of: *Antología personal.*
Paperbound.

BECCO 275

29. Borges, Jorge Luis.

A Personal Anthology. Edited and with a foreword by Anthony Kerrigan. [New York:] Castle Books, [1967].
[i-iv] v-x [xi-xii], 1-210 [211-216] p. 21.5 cm.

English translation of: *Antología personal.*
Reprinted by arrangement with Grove Press.

[BECCO 275]

II. POETRY

30. Abulcásim el Hadramí [pseud.].

"El poeta declara su nombradía." (In: *Los anales de Buenos Aires*, Año I, no. 6, p. 49. Buenos Aires, June 1946).

Pseudonym for Borges. This title was reprinted in *El hacedor*. 2 copies.

31. Almoqtádir el Madrebí [pseud.].

"Cuarteta." (In: *Los anales de Buenos Aires*, Año I, no. 5, p. 50. Buenos Aires, May 1946).

Pseudonym for Borges. This title was reprinted in *El hacedor*. 2 copies.

32. Borges, Jorge Luis.

"A celui qui n'est plus jeune." (In: *Cahiers de L'Herne*, no. 4, p. 80. Paris, 1964).

Appears in "Textes inédits" section. 3 copies.

33. Borges, Jorge Luis.

"A Francisco López Merino." (In: *La vida literaria; crítica, información bibliográfica*, Año I, no. 3, p. 2. Buenos Aires, October 1928).

34. Borges, Jorge Luis.

"Absence." (In: *Cahiers de L'Herne*, no. 4, p. 75. Paris, 1964).

Appears in "Textes inédits" section. 3 copies.

35. Borges, Jorge Luis.

Adrogué. Ilustraciones de Norah Borges. [Adrogué:] Ediciones Adrogué, 1977. [i-iv], [1-6] 7-75 [76] p. 23 cm.

Contains prologue by Roy Bartholomew. 2 copies.

36. Borges, Jorge Luis.

"Aldea." (In: *Prisma; revista mural*, no. 1. Buenos Aires, December 1921).

One of Borges' earliest published poems.

37. Borges, Jorge Luis.

"El ángel." (In: *New Found Land*, Jaargang I, no. 1, p. 37. Amsterdam, September 1981).

38. Borges, Jorge Luis.

"The Angel." (In: *New Found Land*, Jaargang I, no. 1, p. 40. Amsterdam, September 1981).

Translation into English of Borges' poem "El ángel" by Norman Thomas di Giovanni.

39. Borges, Jorge Luis.

"Antelación de amor." (In: *Proa*, Año II, no. 8, p. 38. Buenos Aires, March 1925).

40. Borges, Jorge Luis.

Antología poética, 1923-1977. Madrid: Alianza Editorial, [1981]. [1-6] 7-147 [148-152] p. 18 cm. (El libro de bolsillo. Sección: literatura, 805.)

41. Borges, Jorge Luis.

"Ariosto y los árabes." (In: *Sur*, no. 265, pp. [19]-21. Buenos Aires, July-August 1960).

42. Borges, Jorge Luis.

"Atardecer--Le soir tombé." (In: *Europe*, no. 637, p. [67]. Paris, May 1982).

43. Borges, Jorge Luis.

Ausgewählte Gedichte. Auswahl aus den "Poemas 1923-1958." Deutsch von Otto Wolf. Farbtafeln: Jörg Remé, Amsterdam. München: Wilhelm Heyne Verlag, [1978].
[1-4] 5-149 [150-152] p. 18 cm.
(Heyne-Lyrik, no. 6.)

German translation of: *Poemas, 1923-1958.*

44. Borges, Jorge Luis.

"Buenos Aires." (In: *Cuadernos*, no. 75, p. 10. Paris, August 1963).

45. Borges, Jorge Luis.

"Cambridge." (In: *Sur*, no. 314, pp. [19]-20. Buenos Aires, September-October 1968).

46. Borges, Jorge Luis.

Carme presunto e altre poesie. Introduzione e traduzione di Umberto Cianciòlo. [Milano:] Arnoldo Mondadori Editore, [1980].
[1-5] 6-183 [184-192] p. 18.5 cm.
(Gli Oscar, 1184. Oscar poesia e teatro, 47.)

Italian translation of: *Poemas, 1923-1958.*

[BECCO 296]

47. Borges, Jorge Luis.

La cifra. Buenos Aires: Emecé Editores, [1981].
[1-11] 12-108 [109-112] p. 22 cm.
(Obra poética de Jorge Luis Borges.)

First edition.

48. Borges, Jorge Luis.

Cosmogonías. Jorge Luis Borges. Aldo Sessa. Buenos Aires: Ediciones Librería La Ciudad, [1976].
16 unnumbered leaves [pp. 1-32]. 31 cm.

Copy number 313 of 3,000.

49. Borges, Jorge Luis.

Cuaderno San Martín. Con un retrato a lápiz del autor por Silvina Ocampo. [Buenos Aires: Editorial Proa, 1929].
[1-8] 9-63 [64] p. 19.5 cm.
(Cuadernos del Plata, 2.)

First edition. 2 copies. One copy bound with first edition of *El idioma de los argentinos.* Copy number 226 of 250. Contains bookstamp of L. Galtier. Minor handwritten textual revisions. Contains frontispiece portrait. Second copy (number 179) in a special binding. Contains author's autograph on p. 43: "Jorge Luis Borges." Title page displays ownership stamp of Marcelo Saraví Cisneros.

BECCO 8

50. Borges, Jorge Luis.

Deathwatch on the Southside. Translated by Robert Fitzgerald. Cambridge: The Grolier Book Shop, [1968].
6 unnumbered leaves [pp. 1-12]. 20 cm.

2 copies. One copy is number 101 of 150, signed by the author and the translator. Second copy, also signed, is number 129. Originally published in *Cuaderno San Martín* in 1927, this poem was titled "La noche que en el sur lo velaron."

51. Borges, Jorge Luis.

"Dualidad en una despedida." (In: *Proa*, Año II, no. 8, p. 37. Buenos Aires, March 1925).

52. Borges, Jorge Luis.

Elogio de la sombra. [Buenos Aires:] Emecé, [1969].
[1-8] 9-160 [161-166] p. 23.5 cm.
(Obra poética de Borges.)

2 copies.

BECCO 19

53. Borges, Jorge Luis.

Elogio dell'ombra. Seguito da un "Abbozzo di autobiografia" a cura di Norman Thomas di Giovanni. Versione contesto a fronte de Francesco Tentori Montalto. [Torino:] Einaudi, [1978, c. 1971].
[1-5] 6-197 [198-200] p. 19.5 cm.
(Nuovi coralli, 187.)

Italian translation of: *Elogio de la sombra.*

[BECCO 298]

54. Borges, Jorge Luis.

"De Engel." (In: *New Found Land*, Jaargang I, no. 1, pp. 38-39. Amsterdam, September 1981).

Translation into Dutch of Borges' poem "El ángel," with a critical article by Barber van de Pol.

55. Borges, Jorge Luis.

"De Engel." (In: *New Found Land*, Jaargang I, no. 1, p. 46. Amsterdam, September 1981).

Translation into Dutch of Borges' poem "El ángel" by Robert Lemm.

56. Borges, Jorge Luis.

"De Engel." (In: *New Found Land*, Jaargang I, no. 1, pp. 49-50. Amsterdam, September 1981).

Translation into Dutch of Borges' poem "El ángel," with a critical article by Cees Nootboom. Facsimile of the translated poem in manuscript on preceding page (p. 48).

57. Borges, Jorge Luis.

Fervor de Buenos Aires. Poemas. [Buenos Aires: 1923]. 32 unnumbered leaves [pp. 1-64]. 19 cm.

The first edition of Borges' first book, and extremely rare. Cover designed by Borges' sister Norah. Alderman Library owns two copies of this book. One copy may be made up from proof sheets, since two sets of page numbers have been added, one by hand and the other (using a different numbering) stamped by machine. This copy has a photograph of Borges pasted on the front (volume) flyleaf, which also bears author's autograph: "Jorge Luis Borges." Contains 2 ownership stamps of Lysandro Z. D. Galtier, a friend of Borges in the 1920s and a fellow poet. This copy also features minor handwritten textual revisions. Bound with first editions of

Inquisiciones and *El tamaño de mi esperanza* (external spine height, 18.5 cm.). Second copy is as issued originally. This copy is inscribed: "al Dr. Domingo Sasso/ afectuosamente/ Jorge-Luis Borges."

BECCO 3

58. Borges, Jorge Luis.

Fervor de Buenos Aires. [Buenos Aires:] Emecé, [1969].
[1-8] 9-156 [157-162] p. 23 cm.
(Obra poética de Borges.)

First printing in this form.

BECCO 4

59. Borges, Jorge Luis.

Fervor de Buenos Aires. [Buenos Aires:] Emecé, [1970, c. 1969].
[1-8] 9-156 [157-162] p. 23 cm.
(Obra poética de Borges.)

Second printing in this form.

BECCO 5

60. Borges, Jorge Luis.

"El forastero/ Foreigner." (In: *Artes hispánicas/ Hispanic Arts*, Vol. 1, no. 1, p. 10. New York, Spring/Summer 1967).

Includes recording of Borges and other Latin American poets reading from their works.

61. Borges, Jorge Luis.

"Forjadura." (In: *Proa*, Año I, no. 2, [p. 3]. Buenos Aires, December 1922).

62. Borges, Jorge Luis.

Gedichte, 1923-1965. Buenos Aires mit Inbrunst. Mond gegenüber. Notizheft San Martín. Der Andere, der Selbe. Für die sechs Saiten. Herausgegeben und übersetzt von Gisbert Haefs. [München:] Carl Hanser Verlag, [1982].
[1-6] 7-223 [224-228] p. 19 cm.
(Gesammelte Werke, 1.)

German translations of: *Fervor de Buenos Aires, Luna de enfrente, Cuaderno San Martín, El otro, el mismo*, and *Para las seis cuerdas.*

63. Borges, Jorge Luis.

Gedichte, 1969-1976. Lob des Schattens. Das Gold der Tiger. Die tiefe Rose. Die eiserne Münze. Herausgegeben und übersetzt von Curt Meyer-Clason. [München:] Carl Hanser Verlag, [1980].
[1-6] 7-177 [178-180] p. 19 cm.
(Gesammelte Werke, 2.)

German translations of: *Elogio de la sombra, El oro de los tigres, La rosa profunda*, and *La moneda de hierro.*

64. Borges, Jorge Luis.

Gedichten. Keuze, nawoord, vertaling en noten Robert Lemm. Amsterdam: Uitgeverij De Bezige Bij, 1980.
[1-4] 5-209 [210-212] p. 20 cm.
(BB Poëzie.)

2 copies.

65. Borges, Jorge Luis.

The Gold of the Tigers: Selected Later Poems: A Bilingual Edition. Translated by Alastair Reid. New York: E. P. Dutton, [1977].
[1-5] 6-95 [96] p. 24 cm. (bound)
[1-5] 6-95 [96] p. 23.5 cm. (paper)

Selections with English translations from Borges' *El oro de los tigres* and *La rosa profunda.* First edition. 2 copies, one paperbound.

66. Borges, Jorge Luis.

"Hermanos." (In: *Grecia; revista decenal de literatura,* Año III, no. 45, p. 14. Madrid, 1 July 1920).

Borges' second appearance in print. During his residence in Spain with his family, Borges produced this poem for the short-lived Ultraist periodical *Grecia.* His sister Norah illustrated this issue with two woodcuts, including the cover design. This example bears the following inscription in Norah Borges' hand: "Signor/Armando Bossi - Via Orto Botanico/Varese/ITALIA/997/EXP: NORAH BORGES./HOTEL CONTINENTAL/PALMA DE MALLORCA/ESPANA."

67. Borges, Jorge Luis.

Historia de la noche. [Buenos Aires:] Emecé Editores, [1977].
[1-12] 13-148 [149-156] p. 23 cm.
(Obra poética de Borges.)

68. Borges, Jorge Luis.

"Inscription pour un sépulcre." (In: *Cahiers de L'Herne,* no. 4, p. 80. Paris, 1964).

Appears in "Textes inédits" section. 3 copies.

69. Borges, Jorge Luis.

"Insomnio." (In: *Sur*, Año VI, no. 27, pp. [71]-72. Buenos Aires, December 1936).

70. Borges, Jorge Luis.

"Le jour se lève." (In: *Cahiers de L'Herne*, no. 4, p. 76. Paris, 1964).

Appears in "Textes inédits" section. 3 copies.

71. Borges, Jorge Luis.

"The Keeper." (In: *The New Yorker*, Vol. LIII, no. 29, p. 26. New York, 5 September 1977).

Translated from the Spanish by Alastair Reid.

72. Borges, Jorge Luis.

Límites. Buenos Aires: [Francisco A. Colombo,] 1958.
[1-8] 9-24 [25-32] p. 33 cm.

Number 139 of 150 copies. Published for the friends of Frank M. Virasoro and Federico M. Vogelius. Contains bookplate of Miguel de Torre.

BECCO 141

73. Borges, Jorge Luis.

Lob des Schattens. Gedichte. Aus dem Spanischen von Curt Meyer-Clason. [München:] Carl Hanser Verlag, [1971].
[1-4] 5-60 p. 22.5 cm.

German translation of: *Elogio de la sombra*.

BECCO 245

74. Borges, Jorge Luis.

Lof der duisternis. [Rotterdam:] Flamboyant/P, [1977].
[1-6] 7-84 p. 20.5 cm.
(Flamboyant perspektief.)

Dutch translation of: *Elogio de la sombra*.

75. Borges, Jorge Luis.

"Lucas, XXIII." (In: *Sur*, no. 268, p. 69. Buenos Aires, January-February 1961).

76. Borges, Jorge Luis.

"La luna." (In: *Sur*, no. 260, pp. [13]-15. Buenos Aires, September-October 1959).

77. Borges, Jorge Luis.

Luna de enfrente. Versos de Jorje [sic] Luis Borges. Buenos Aires: Editorial Proa, 1925.
[1-8] 9-42 [43-44] p. 29 cm.

Scarcest of Borges' first editions. Alderman Library owns two copies. One copy is number 142 of 300. This copy contains author's autograph inscription: "Para La Nación--homenaje de Jorge Luis Borges." Second copy is unnumbered. This copy bears author's autograph (in a much later example): "Jorge Luis Borges." This copy lacks first leaf [pp. 1-2]. Both copies contain a textual correction in Borges' hand on p. 37.

BECCO 6

78. Borges, Jorge Luis.

Luna de enfrente y Cuaderno San Martín. [Buenos Aires:] Emecé, [1969].

[1-16] 17-128 [129-?] p. 23 cm.
(Obra poética de Borges.)

Imperfect copy, with pages missing at end of volume. Index title page glued down to rear cover.

BECCO 7

79. Borges, Jorge Luis.

"Mayo 20, 1928." (In: *Sur*, no. 316-317, pp. [1]-2. Buenos Aires, January-April 1969).

80. Borges, Jorge Luis.

La moneda de hierro. [Buenos Aires:] Emecé, [1976].
[1-8] 9-162 [163-170] p. 23.5 cm.
(Obra poética de Borges.)

2 copies.

81. Borges, Jorge Luis.

La moneta de ferro. A cura di Cesco Vian. [Milano:] Rizzoli, [1981].
[1-4] 5-159 [160-168] p. 22.5 cm.
(La scala: il catalogo.)

First edition. Italian translation of: *La moneda de hierro*.

82. Borges, Jorge Luis.

"La noche de San Juan." (In: *Proa*, Año I, no. 1, p. [4]. Buenos Aires, August 1922).

83. Borges, Jorge Luis.

Nueve poemas. Buenos Aires: [Ediciones "El Mangrullo,"] 1955.
[1-10] 11-32 [33-44] p. 29.5 cm.

Number XII of 50 copies. Contains author's autograph: "Jorge Luis Borges." Includes an original lithograph laid in, by Santiago Cogerno. Printed by Francisco A. Colombo.

BECCO 139

84. Borges, Jorge Luis.

Obra poética, 1923-1964. [Buenos Aires:] Emecé Editòres, [1964].
[i-ii], [1-16] 17-279 [280-284] p. 20.5 cm.

Special edition commemorating the 25th anniversary of the founding of Emecé Editores. Fourth edition of the *Obra poética.*

2 copies. One copy contains partly illegible inscription by Borges' mother: "Para nuestro [querido?]/[?]/Leonor." Below this inscription is the author's autograph: "Jorge Luis Borges."

BECCO 14

85. Borges, Jorge Luis.

Obra poética, 1923-1966. [Buenos Aires:] Emecé Editores, [1966, c. 1964].
[1-16] 17-335 [336] p. 19 cm.
(Obras completas.)

BECCO 17

86. Borges, Jorge Luis.

Obra poética, 1923-1969. [Buenos Aires:] Emecé Editores, [1972].
[1-14] 15-419 [420-424] p. 18.5 cm.
(Obras completas.)

Ninth edition.

87. Borges, Jorge Luis.

Obra poética, 1923-1976. Buenos Aires: Emecé Editores, [1978, c. 1977].
[1-14] 15-514 [515-520] p. 21.5 cm.

Tenth printing. 2 copies.

88. Borges, Jorge Luis.

Oeuvre poétique (1925-1965). Mise en vers français par Ibarra. [Paris:] Gallimard, [1970].
[1-6] 7-215 [216-224] p. 20.5 cm.
(Du monde entier.)

French translation of: *Obra poética.* 2 copies.

BECCO 261

89. Borges, Jorge Luis.

Oeuvre poétique, 1925-1965. Mise en vers français par Ibarra. [Paris:] Gallimard, [1983, c. 1970].
[1-6] 7-215 [216-224] p. 20.5 cm.
(Du monde entier.)

French translation of: *Obra poética.*

[BECCO 261]

90. Borges, Jorge Luis.

L'or des tigres. L'autre, le même II. Eloge de l'ombre. Ferveur de Buenos Aires. Advertissement, notes et mise en vers français par Ibarra. [Paris:] Gallimard, [1976].
[3-6] 7-254 [255-258] p. 20.5 cm.
(Du monde entier.)

French translations of: *El oro de los tigres, El otro, el mismo, Elogio de la sombra,* and *Fervor de Buenos Aires.*

91. Borges, Jorge Luis.

El oro de los tigres. [Buenos Aires:] Emecé, [1972].
[1-9] 10-168 [169-174] p. 23 cm.
(Obra poética de Borges.)

First edition. 2 copies.

BECCO 24

92. Borges, Jorge Luis.

El otro, el mismo. [Buenos Aires:] Emecé, [1969].
[1-8] 9-263 [264-274] p. 23 cm.
(Obra poética de Borges.)

BECCO 22

93. Borges, Jorge Luis.

"Page écrite à la mémoire du Colonel Suárez vainqueur à Junín." (In: *Cahiers de L'Herne*, no. 4, p. 78. Paris, 1964).

Appears in "Textes inédits" section. 3 copies.

94. Borges, Jorge Luis.

"Página para recordar al Coronel Suárez, vencedor en Junín." (In: *Sur*, no. 226, pp. 47-48. Buenos Aires, January-February 1954).

2 copies.

95. Borges, Jorge Luis.

"The Palace." (In: *The New Yorker*, Vol. LIII, no. 32, p. 38. New York, 26 September 1977).

Translated from the Spanish by Alastair Reid.

96. Borges, Jorge Luis.

Para las seis cuerdas. Ilustrado por Héctor Basaldúa. [Buenos Aires:] Emecé Editores, [1965]. 30 unnumbered leaves [pp. 1-60]. 36 cm.

First edition. 3 copies, one clothbound (34 cm.).

BECCO 15

97. Borges, Jorge Luis.

Para las seis cuerdas; milongas de Jorge Luis Borges. Ilustrado por Héctor Basaldúa. [Buenos Aires:] Emecé, [1970, c. 1965].
35 unnumbered leaves [pp. 1-70]. 26.5 cm.

Second edition. 2 copies.

BECCO 16

98. Borges, Jorge Luis.

"Paradiso, XXXI, 108." (In: *Sur*, no. 231, pp. [1]-2. Buenos Aires, November-December 1954).

99. Borges, Jorge Luis.

Poemas, 1922-1943. Buenos Aires: Editorial Losada, S.A., [1943].
[1-10] 11-181 [182-184] p. 21 cm.
(Poetas de España y América.)

First edition. 3 copies.

BECCO 9

100. Borges, Jorge Luis.

Poemas, 1923-1953. [Buenos Aires:] Emecé Editores, S.A., [1954].
[1-12] 13-174 [175-176] p. 19 cm.

(Obras completas, 2.)

First edition. 2 copies.

BECCO 10

101. Borges, Jorge Luis.

"Poème conjectural." (In: *Cahiers de L'Herne*, no. 4, p. 77. Paris, 1964).

Appears in "Textes inédits" section. 3 copies.

102. Borges, Jorge Luis.

"Poème des dons." (In: *Cahiers de L'Herne*, no. 4, pp. 79-80. Paris, 1964).

Appears in "Textes inédits" section. 3 copies.

103. Borges, Jorge Luis.

Poems. Translated and with a note by Anthony Kerrigan. Dublin: New Writers' Press, 1969.
[i-ii], [1-6] 7-23 [24-26] p. 26 cm.

Number 149 of 300 copies.

104. Borges, Jorge Luis.

Poesías. Selección, estudio preliminar y notas de María Adela Renard. Buenos Aires: Editorial Kapelusz, [1977].
[1-10] 11-180 [181-192] p. 16.5 cm.
(Grandes obras de la literatura universal, 140.)

2 copies.

105. Borges, Jorge Luis.

La rosa profunda. [Buenos Aires:] Emecé, [1975].
[1-8] 9-162 [163-170] p. 23.5 cm.

First edition.

106. Borges, Jorge Luis.

Rosa y azul. La rosa de Paracelso. Tigres Azules.
Ilustraciones de Alfredo González. [Madrid:]
Sedmay Ediciones, [1977].
34 unnumbered leaves [pp. 1-68]. 31 cm.

First edition.

107. Borges, Jorge Luis.

Rose et bleu. [Paris:] Editions de la Différence,
[1978].
[1-12] 13-106 [107-112] p. 20 cm.
("Cantos.")

French translation of: *Rosa y azul.*

108. Borges, Jorge Luis.

La rose profonde. La monnaie de fer. Histoire de la nuit. Avertissement, notes et mise en vers français par Ibarra. [Paris:] Gallimard, [1983].
[1-6] 7-193 [194-200] p. 20.5 cm.
(Du monde entier.)

French translations of: *La rosa profunda*, *La moneda de hierro*, and *Historia de la noche.*

109. Borges, Jorge Luis.

"Salmos." (In: *Proa*, Año I, no. 1, pp. 49-51.
Buenos Aires, August 1924).

110. Borges, Jorge Luis.

"Sarmiento." (In: *Sur*, no. 273, pp. [1]-2. Buenos Aires, November-December 1961).

111. Borges, Jorge Luis.

Seis composiciones. Buenos Aires: Francisco A. Colombo, [1960].
[1-6] 7-36 [37-40] p. 36.5 cm.

Number 21 of 50 copies. Published for the friends of Federico M. Vogelius, this copy was printed for Miguel Lermon.

BECCO 144

112. Borges, Jorge Luis.

Seis poemas escandinavos. Ilustraciones de Juan Carlos Benítez. Buenos Aires: [Francisco A. Colombo, 1966].
[1-10] 11-23 [24-32] p. 19.5 cm.

One of 50 copies. This copy printed for Horacio Esteban Ratti. Initialed by the printer, Colombo.

BECCO 148

113. Borges, Jorge Luis.

Selected Poems, 1923-1967. Edited with an introduction and notes by Norman Thomas di Giovanni. [New York:] Delacorte Press/Seymour Lawrence, [1972].
[1 unnumbered leaf], [i-viii] ix-xxviii [xxix-xxxii], [1] 2-328 [329-334] p. 23.5 cm.

Translations into English by Ben Belitt, Robert Fitzgerald, W. S. Merwin, Alastair Reid, John Updike, and others.

BECCO 284

114. Borges, Jorge Luis.

Selected Poems, 1923-1967. Edited with an introduction and notes by Norman Thomas di Giovanni. [London:] Allen Lane/The Penguin Press, [1972].
[i-vi] vii-xxv [xxvi], [1] 2-348 [349-350] p. 24 cm.

[BECCO 284]

115. Borges, Jorge Luis.

"Seventeen Haiku." (In: *The New Republic*, no. 3,537, p. 30. Washington, 1 November 1982).

Translations into English by Norman Thomas di Giovanni. Gift of James M. Campbell.

116. Borges, Jorge Luis.

Siete poemas sajones. Seven Saxon Poems. Impressions by Arnaldo Pomodoro. [Verona:] Plain Wrapper Press, [1974].
[i-iv], [1-8] 9-37 [38-44] p. 39.5 cm.
(Escritores panamericanos, 1.)

"This edition, limited to one hundred copies numbered in Arabic and twenty in Roman, was printed on a Washington handpress by Richard - Gabriel Rummonds . . . This book is copy number 21."

With 8 blind-embossed impressions in the text, and three low-relief, gold plated bronzes by Arnaldo Pomodoro glued and nailed to the top. Signed by Borges and Pomodoro. Borges' most impressive work from the standpoint of the printer's art.

117. Borges, Jorge Luis.

"Sonetos." (In: *Sur*, no. 251, pp. [1]-3. Buenos Aires, March-April 1958).

118. Borges, Jorge Luis.

"Susana Bombal." (In: *Revista de Occidente*, no. 100, p. [7]. Madrid, July 1971).

119. Borges, Jorge Luis.

"El tango." (In: *Sur*, no. 253, pp. [1]-3. Buenos Aires, July-August 1958).

120. Borges, Jorge Luis.

"Texas." (In: *Sur*, no. 275, p. [14]. Buenos Aires, March-April 1962).

121. Borges, Jorge Luis.

Treize poèms de J. L. Borges. Traduits par Roger Caillois. Illustrées par Pierre Alechinsky. [Montpellier:] Fata Morgana, [1978].
32 unnumbered leaves [pp. 1-64]. 22.5 cm.
(Dioscures.)

Number 45 of 60 special copies, with two original eaux-fortes by Alechinsky.

122. Borges, Jorge Luis.

"Versos para Fernán Silva Valdéz." (In: *Proa*, Año II, no. 14, p. 16. Buenos Aires, December 1925).

123. Camerarius, Gaspar [pseud.].

"Le regret d'Héraclite." (In: *Los anales de Buenos Aires*, Año I, no. 10, p. 55. Buenos Aires, October 1946).

Pseudonym for Borges. This title was reprinted in *El hacedor*.

124. Gering, H. [pseud.].

"El enemigo generoso." (In: *Los anales de Buenos Aires*, Año I, no. 10, p. 56. Buenos Aires, October 1946).

Pseudonym for Borges. This title was reprinted in *El hacedor*.

125. *Hojas de poesía*, no. 20 [Buenos Aires: 1976]. 2 unnumbered leaves [pp. 1-4]. 29 cm.

Contains poems by Borges from earlier publications, and a short biographical sketch. 2 copies.

126. Lynch Davis, B. [pseud.].

"Museo." (In: *Los anales de Buenos Aires*, Año I, no. 3, pp. 53-56. Buenos Aires, March 1946).

Pseudonym for Borges. 10 passages appear in this section, which is unsigned, in this first issue to feature the "Museo" pages. 2 copies.

127. Lynch Davis, B. [pseud.].

"Museo." (In: *Los anales de Buenos Aires*, Año I, no. 4, pp. 45-47. Buenos Aires, April 1946).

6 passages appear in this section. 2 copies.

128. Lynch Davis, B. [pseud.].

"Museo." (In: *Los anales de Buenos Aires*. Año I, no. 5, pp. 50-52. Buenos Aires, May 1946).

11 passages appear in this section. 2 copies.

129. Lynch Davis, B. [pseud.].

"Museo." (In: *Los anales de Buenos Aires*, Año I, no. 6, pp. 49-51. Buenos Aires, June 1946).

14 passages appear in this section. 2 copies.

130. Lynch Davis, B. [pseud.].

"Museo." (In: *Los anales de Buenos Aires*, Año I, no. 7, pp. 60-62. Buenos Aires, July 1946).

11 passages appear in this section. 2 copies.

131. Lynch Davis, B. [pseud.].

"Museo." (In: *Los anales de Buenos Aires*, Año I, no. 8, pp. 52-54. Buenos Aires, August 1946).

18 passages appear in this section. 2 copies.

132. Lynch Davis, B. [pseud.].

"Museo." (In: *Los anales de Buenos Aires*, Año I, no. 9, pp. 63-64. Buenos Aires, September 1946).

9 passages appear in this section. 2 copies.

133. Lynch Davis, B. [pseud.].

"Museo." (In: *Los anales de Buenos Aires*, Año I, no. 10, pp. 55-56. Buenos Aires, October 1946).

11 passages appear in this section. 2 copies.

134. Lynch Davis, B. [pseud.].

"Museo." (In: *Los anales de Buenos Aires*, Año I, no. 11, pp. 60-62. Buenos Aires, December 1946).

16 passages appear in this section. 2 copies.

135. Platero Haedo, Julio [pseud.].

"Límites." (In: *Los anales de Buenos Aires*, Año I, no. 5, p. 50. Buenos Aires, May 1946).

Pseudonym for Borges. This title was reprinted in *El hacedor*. 2 copies.

136. Suárez Miranda [pseud.].

"Del rigor en la ciencia." (In: *Los anales de Buenos Aires*, Año I, no. 3, p. 53. Buenos Aires, March 1946).

Pseudonym for Borges, whose article appears in "Museo" section. This title was reprinted in *El hacedor*. 2 copies.

III. ESSAYS

137. Borges, Jorge Luis.

"Acotación del árbol en la lírica." (In: *Proa*, Año II, no. 10, pp. 58-59. Buenos Aires, May 1925).

138. Borges, Jorge Luis.

"Acotaciones." (In: *Proa*, Año I, no. 1, pp. 30-32. Buenos Aires, August 1924).

139. Borges, Jorge Luis.

"Adolfo Bioy: 'Antes del novecientos'." (In: *Sur*, no. 257, pp. [61]-62. Buenos Aires, March-April 1959).

Article appearing in "Notas" section, under heading "Los libros."

140. Borges, Jorge Luis.

"Ainsworth Noyes: 'Christopher Smart'." (In: *Los anales de Buenos Aires*, Año I, no. 4, pp. 59-60. Buenos Aires, April 1946).

Article appearing in "Libros" section. 2 copies.

141. Borges, Jorge Luis.

"Alfonso Reyes." (In: *Sur*, no. 264, p. [1]-2. Buenos Aires, May-June 1960).

142. Borges, Jorge Luis.

"Alfonso Reyes: 'Reloj del sol'." (In: *Síntesis*, Año I, no. 1, pp. 110-114. Buenos Aires, June 1927).

Article appearing in “Bibliografía y notas” section.

143. Borges, Jorge Luis.

“Américo Castro: ‘La peculiaridad linguística rioplatense y su sentido histórico’.” (In: *Sur*, Año X, no. 86, pp. [66]-70. Buenos Aires, November 1941).

Article appearing in “Notas” section, under heading “Los libros.”

144. Borges, Jorge Luis.

“‘Los amigos dilectos’, Ricardo Sáenz Hayes, Gleizer, 1927 Buenos Aires.” (In: *Síntesis*, Año I, no. 2, pp. 121-122. Buenos Aires, July 1927).

Article appearing in “Bibliografía” section.

145. Borges, Jorge Luis.

“La amortajada.” (In: *Sur*, Año VIII, no. 47, pp. 80-81. Buenos Aires, August 1938).

Article appearing in “Notas” section, under heading “Letras hispanoamericanas.”

146. Borges, Jorge Luis.

“Análisis del último capítulo del *Quijote*.” (In: *Revista de la Universidad de Buenos Aires*, V Epoca, Año 1, no. 1, pp. [3]-11. Buenos Aires, January-March 1956).

Offprint of the original article.

[BECCO 73]

147. Borges, Jorge Luis.

"Anotación al 23 de agosto de 1944." (In: *Sur*, Año XIV, no. 120, pp. [24]-26. Buenos Aires, October 1944).

148. Borges, Jorge Luis.

"La apostasía de Coifí." (In: *Entregas de la licorne*, Segunda Epoca, Año I, no. 1-2, pp. 45-48. Montevideo, November 1953).

2 copies.

149. Borges, Jorge Luis.

Aspectos de la literatura gauchesca. Montevideo: Número, 1950.
[1-4] 5-35 [36] p. 21.5 cm.

2 copies. One copy is number 743 of 1,000 copies. Second copy is number 493.

BECCO 68

150. Borges, Jorge Luis.

"Atavares de la tortuga." (In: *Sur*, Año IX, no. 63, pp. [18]-23. Buenos Aires, December 1939).

151. Borges, Jorge Luis.

"Bibliografía." (In: *Proa*, Año I, no. 2, pp. [4-5]. Buenos Aires, December 1922).

152. Borges, Jorge Luis.

"Bibliographie." (In: *La revue argentine*, 2e Année, no. 15, pp. [54]-56. Paris, April-May 1936).

153. Borges, Jorge Luis.

"El caso Lolita." (In: *Sur*, no. 260, pp. 49-50. Buenos Aires, September-October 1959).

Article appearing in "Crónicas" section.

154. Borges, Jorge Luis.

Conférences. Traduit de l'espagnol par Françoise Rosset. [Paris:] Gallimard, [1985].
[1-6] 7-215 [216-224] p. 18 cm.
(Collection folio/essais, 2.)

French translations of: *Siete noches* and *Borges, oral.*

155. Borges, Jorge Luis.

"El Coronel Ascasubi." (In: *Sur*, Año I, no. 1, pp. [129]-140. Buenos Aires, Summer 1931).

Number 83 of 100 copies. First issue of Victoria Ocampo's celebrated and long-lived literary magazine. Borges contributed regularly to this periodical for many years.

156. Borges, Jorge Luis.

"La criolledá en Ipuche." (In: *Proa*, Año I, no. 3, pp. 27-29. Buenos Aires, October 1924).

2 copies.

157. Borges, Jorge Luis.

De cultus van het boek en andere essays. Vertaling en naawoord Barber van de Pol. Amsterdam: Uitgeverij De Bezige Bij, 1981.
[1-6] 7-254 [255-256] p. 20 cm.
(Leven & letteren.)

Dutch translation of: *Otras inquisiciones.* 2 copies.

158. Borges, Jorge Luis.

"Une curieuse méthode." (In: *Cahiers de L'Herne*, no. 4, pp. 94-95. Paris, 1964).

Appears in "Textes inédits" section. 3 copies.

159. Borges, Jorge Luis.

"Un curioso método." (In: *Ficción*, no. 6, pp. [55]-56. Buenos Aires, March-April 1957).

160. Borges, Jorge Luis.

"De alguien a nadie." (In: *Sur*, Año XVIII, no. 185, pp. [7]-9. Buenos Aires, March 1950).

161. Borges, Jorge Luis.

"De Jorge Luis Borges." (In: *Nosotros*, Segunda Epoca, Año I, no. 1, pp. 60-61. Buenos Aires, April 1936).

162. Borges, Jorge Luis.

"'De regreso,' film." (In: *Sur*, Año VII, no. 38, pp. 92-93. Buenos Aires, November 1937).

Article appearing in "Cine" section.

163. Borges, Jorge Luis.

"Debats de 'Sur'." (In: *Cahiers de L'Herne*, no. 4, pp. 92-93. Paris, 1964).

Appears in "Textes inédits" section. 3 copies.

164. Borges, Jorge Luis.

"Défense de Bouvard et Pécuchet." (In: *Cahiers de L'Herne*, no. 4, pp. 85-88. Paris, 1964).

Appears in "Textes inédits" section. 3 copies.

165. Borges, Jorge Luis.

"Défense de la Cabale." (In: *Cahiers de L'Herne*, no. 4, pp. 89-91. Paris, 1964).

Appears in "Textes inédits" section. 3 copies.

166. Borges, Jorge Luis.

"Después de las imágenes." (In: *Proa*, Año I, no. 5, pp. 22-23. Buenos Aires, December 1924).

167. Borges, Jorge Luis.

"Destino escandinavo." (In: *Sur*, no. 219-220, pp. 9-13. Buenos Aires, January-February 1953).

168. Borges, Jorge Luis.

"Deux films." (In: *Cahiers de L'Herne*, no. 4, p. 97. Paris, 1964).

Appears in "Textes inédits" section. 3 copies.

169. Borges, Jorge Luis.

"Deux notes bibliographiques." (In: *Cahiers de L'Herne*, no. 4, pp. 98-99. Paris, 1964).

Contains two bibliographic notes: “Francisco Soto y Calvo” and “Juan Carlos Welker.” Appears in “Textes inédits” section. 3 copies.

170. Borges, Jorge Luis.

Discusión. Buenos Aires: M. Gleizer, Editor, 1932.
[1-8] 9-161 [162-168] p. 19.5 cm.
(Colección de nuevos escritores argentinos.)

First edition. 3 copies. One copy contains Borges' autograph inscription on p. [1]: “Jorge Luis Borges.” Special binding (spine height 18.5 cm. on this copy). Second copy contains autograph on p. [1]: “a Paco Luis, con un abrazo verdadero de Georgie.” Third copy is not signed.

BECCO 60

171. Borges, Jorge Luis.

Discusión. [Buenos Aires:] Emecé Editores, S.A., [1957].
[1-8] 9-180 [181-188] p. 18.5 cm.
(Obras completas, 6.)

BECCO 61

172. Borges, Jorge Luis.

Discusión. [Buenos Aires:] Emecé Editores, [1964, c. 1957].
[1-8] 9-180 [181-192] p. 18.5 cm.
(Obras completas, 6.)

Third printing.

[BECCO 62]

173. Borges, Jorge Luis.

Discusión. [Buenos Aires:] Emecé Editores, [1966, c. 1957].
[1-8] 9-180 [181-192] p. 18.5 cm.
(Obras completas, 6.)

Fourth printing.

[BECCO 62]

174. Borges, Jorge Luis.

Discusión. [Buenos Aires:] Emecé Editores, [1975, c. 1964].
[1-8] 9-180 [181-192] p. 18.5 cm.
(Obras completas.)

Eighth printing.

[BECCO 62]

175. Borges, Jorge Luis.

"Dos films." (In: *Sur*, Año VII, no. 31, pp. 100-101. Buenos Aires, April 1937).

Article appearing in "Notas" section, under the heading "Cine."

176. Borges, Jorge Luis.

"Dudley Fitts: *An Anthology of Contemporary Latin American Poetry.*" (In: *Sur*, Año XII, no. 102, pp. [62]-65. Buenos Aires, March 1943).

Article appearing in "Notas" section, under heading "Los libros."

177. Borges, Jorge Luis.

"Ejercicio de análisis." (In: *Proa*, Año II, no. 14, p. 46. Buenos Aires, December 1925).

178. Borges, Jorge Luis.

Enquêtes 1937-1952. Traduit de l'espagnol par Paul et Sylvia Bénichou. [Paris:] Gallimard, [1978, c. 1957].
[1-9] 10-310 [311-312] p. 18.5 cm.
(Du monde entier.)

French translation of: *Otras inquisiciones*.

[BECCO 250]

179. Borges, Jorge Luis.

"El escritor argentino y la tradición." (In: *Sur*, no. 232, pp. [1]-8. Buenos Aires, January-February 1955).

180. Borges, Jorge Luis.

"El escritor argentino y la tradición." (In: *Sur*, no. 329, pp. [223]-230. Buenos Aires, July-December 1971).

181. Borges, Jorge Luis.

"El espejo de los enigmas." (In: *Sur*, Año X, no. 66, pp. [74]-77. Buenos Aires, March 1940).

Article appearing in "Notas" section.

182. Borges, Jorge Luis.

Essays, 1932-1936. Übersetzt von Karl August Horst, Curt Meyer-Clason, Melanie Walz. Nachwort von Iso Camartin. [München:] Carl Hanser Verlag, [1981].
[1-6] 7-308. 19 cm.
(Gesammelte Werke, 5/I.)

German translation of: *Obras completas.*

183. Borges, Jorge Luis.

Essays, 1952-1979. Übersetzt von Karl August Horst, Curt Meyer-Clason, Gisbert Haefs. Nachwort von Michael Krüger. [München:] Carl Hanser Verlag, [1981].
[1-6] 7-318 [319-320] p. 19 cm.
(Gesammelte Werke, 5/II.)

German translations of: *Obras completas* and *Borges, oral.*

184. Borges, Jorge Luis.

"Estoy milagrosamente vivo." (In: *Clarín: cultura y nación*, p. 3. Buenos Aires, 23 August 1979).

Gift of C. Jared Loewenstein.

185. Borges, Jorge Luis.

"La eternidad y T. S. Eliot (fragmento)." (In: *Poesía; revista internacional de poesía*, no. 3, pp. [3]-7. Buenos Aires, July 1933).

186. Borges, Jorge Luis.

Evaristo Carriego. Buenos Aires: M. Gleizer--Editor, 1930.
[1-8] 9-118 [119-128] p. 18.5 cm.

First edition. Contains frontispiece portrait and 3 additional plates in text. 3 copies. One copy has 2 frontispiece portraits mistakenly bound in. This copy also contains miscellaneous handwritten notes on 2 final blank leaves, including fragments of poetry . . . "Si tus besos me despiertan/ bésame que estoy dormido . . . " Second copy has special binding. Third copy bound in original wrappers with no other special features.

BECCO 57

187. Borges, Jorge Luis.

Evaristo Carriego. Traduit de l'espagnol par Françoise-Marie Rosset. Paris: Editions du Seuil, [1969].
[1-4] 5-158 [159-160] p. 18.5 cm.

French translation of: *Evaristo Carriego.*

BECCO 260

188. Borges, Jorge Luis.

Evaristo Carriego. Madrid: Alianza Editorial/ Buenos Aires: Emecé Editores, [1976].
[1-8] 9-131 [132-136] p. 18 cm.
(El libro de bolsillo; Sección: literatura, 628.)

[BECCO 59]

189. Borges, Jorge Luis.

"La fama." (In: *Clarín: cultura y nación*, p. 1. Buenos Aires, 23 August 1979).

Gift of C. Jared Loewenstein.

190. Borges, Jorge Luis.

"El Fausto criollo." (In: *Proa*, Año II, no. 11, pp. 27-30. Buenos Aires, June 1925).

191. Borges, Jorge Luis.

"Film and Theatre." (In: *Sur*, Año VI, no. 27, pp. [112]-113. Buenos Aires, December 1936).

Article appearing in "Notas" section, under the heading "Letras inglesas."

192. Borges, Jorge Luis.

"Films." (In: *Sur*, Año I, no. 3, pp. 171-173. Buenos Aires, Winter 1931).

193. Borges, Jorge Luis.

"Francisco Ayala: 'El hechizado'." (In: *Sur*, Año XIV, no. 122, pp. [58]-59. Buenos Aires, December 1944).

Article appearing in "Notas" section, under heading "Los libros."

194. Borges, Jorge Luis.

Geschichte der Ewigkeit. München: Carl Hanser, [1965].
[1-4] 5-178 [179-180] p. 21 cm.

German translations of: *Historia de la eternidad, Discusión*, and *Otras inquisiciones*, by Karl August Horst.

BECCO 242

195. Borges, Jorge Luis.

"La grande muraille et les livres." (In: *Cahiers de L'Herne*, no. 4, pp. 81-82. Paris, 1964).

Appears in "Textes inédits" section. 3 copies.

196. Borges, Jorge Luis.

"H. G. Wells: *Travels of a Republican Radical in Search of Hot Water.*" (In: *Sur*, Año X, no. 64, pp. [84]-85. Buenos Aires, January 1940).

Article appearing in "Notas" section, under heading "Los libros."

197. Borges, Jorge Luis.

"Herwarth Walden." (In: *Proa*, Año I, no. 1, p. 21. Buenos Aires, August 1924).

198. Borges, Jorge Luis.

"Hilda Roderick Ellis: 'The Road to Hell'." (In: *Los anales de Buenos Aires*, Año I, no. 3, pp. 62-63. Buenos Aires, March 1946).

Article appearing in "Libros" section. 2 copies.

199. Borges, Jorge Luis.

Historia de la eternidad. [Buenos Aires:] Emecé Editores, [1966, c. 1953].
[1-8] 9-157 [158-160] p. 19 cm.
(Obras completas, 1.)

Fourth impression.

[BECCO 65]

200. Borges, Jorge Luis.

Historia de la eternidad. Madrid: Alianza Editorial/ Buenos Aires: Emecé Editores, [1971].
[1-10] 11-159 [160] p. 18 cm.
(El libro de bolsillo; Sección: literatura, 338.)

BECCO 66

201. Borges, Jorge Luis.

Historia de la eternidad. [Buenos Aires:] Emecé Editores, [1975, c. 1953].
[1-8] 9-156 [157-160] p. 18.5 cm.
(Obras completas.)

Tenth printing.

[BECCO 65]

202. Borges, Jorge Luis.

"Historias de jinetes." (In: *Comentario*, Año I, no. 2, pp. 36-38. Buenos Aires, January-March 1954).

203. Borges, Jorge Luis.

"L'Hydre de Lerne." (In: *Cahiers de L'Herne*, no. 4, p. 100. Paris, 1964).

Appears in "Textes inédits" section. 3 copies.

204. Borges, Jorge Luis.

El idioma de los argentinos. Buenos Aires: M. Gleizer-Editor, 1928.
[1-6] 7-185 [186-196] p. 19.5 cm.
(Colección índice.)

First edition. 2 copies, one bound with first edition of *Cuaderno San Martín.* Contains bookstamp of L. Galtier. Numerous minor handwritten textual revisions. The second copy is in original wrappers with no special features.

BECCO 52

205. Borges, Jorge Luis.

"El idioma infinito." (In: *Proa*, Año II, no. 12, pp. 43-46. Buenos Aires, July 1925).

206. Borges, Jorge Luis.

"Indagación de la palabra, I." (In: *Síntesis*, Año I, no. 1, pp. 69-76. Buenos Aires, June 1927).

207. Borges, Jorge Luis.

"Indagación de la palabra, II." (In: *Síntesis*, Año I, no. 3, pp. 53-57. Buenos Aires, August 1927).

2 copies.

208. Borges, Jorge Luis.

"La inocencia de Layamón." (In: *Sur*, no. 197, pp. 18-21. Buenos Aires, March 1951).

2 copies.

209. Borges, Jorge Luis.

Inquisiciones. Buenos Aires: Editorial Proa, 1925. [1-4] 5-160 [161-162] p. 19 cm.

First and only edition. Borges never allowed this work to be republished. 2 copies. One copy is number 89 of 505 copies. Contains ownership stamp of Lysandro Z. D. Galtier, and bookstore stamp: "Pallas." Minor handwritten textual revisions. Bound with first editions of *Fervor de Buenos Aires* and *El tamaño de mi esperanza*. Prospectus for book, consisting of 2 leaves, bound after p. [2]. Missing pp. [163-164], including colophon. This copy measures 18.5 cm. Second copy is number 281. Contains inscription: "al compañero Varela, muy/cordialmente--Jorge Luis Borges."

BECCO 50

210. Borges, Jorge Luis.

"Interpretación de Silva Valdés." (In: *Proa*, Año I, no. 2, pp. 24-26. Buenos Aires, September 1924).

2 copies.

211. Borges, Jorge Luis.

"Israel." (In: *Sur*, no. 254, pp. [1]-2. Buenos Aires, September-October 1958).

Article appearing in "Testimonio argentino" section. 2 copies.

212. Borges, Jorge Luis.

"John Donne: *Biathanatos*." (In: *Sur*, Año XVII, no. 159, pp. 105-108. Buenos Aires, January 1948).

Article appearing in "Notas" section, under heading "Libros."

213. Borges, Jorge Luis.

"Jorge Luis Borges über Film." (In: *Filmkritik*, 24. Jahrgang, 9. Heft, 285. Heft der Gesamtfolge, pp. 380-419. Berlin, September 1980).

Includes articles on film previously published in *Sur* between 1931 and 1945, here translated into German.

214. Borges, Jorge Luis.

"Juan Ramón-Jiménez." (In: *La torre*, Año V, no. 19-20, pp. 19-20. San Juan, July-December 1957).

215. Borges, Jorge Luis.

"Jules Supervielle." (In: *Sur*, no. 266, p. [2]. Buenos Aires, September-October 1960).

216. Borges, Jorge Luis.

Las Kennigar. Buenos Aires: Francisco A. Colombo, 1933.
[i-ii], [1-6] 7-26 [27-30] p. 24.5 cm.

BECCO 63

217. Borges, Jorge Luis.

"Lawrence y la *Odisea*." (In: *Sur*, Año VI, no. 25, pp. 79-81. Buenos Aires, October 1936).

Article appearing in "Notas" section.

218. Borges, Jorge Luis.

"Leopoldo Lugones." (In: *Sur*, Año VIII, no. 41, pp. [57]-58. Buenos Aires, February 1938).

Article appearing in "Notas" section, under heading "Letras hispanoamericanas."

219. Borges, Jorge Luis.

"Leslie D. Weatherhead: *After Death*." (In: *Sur*, Año XII, no. 105, pp. 83-85. Buenos Aires, July 1943).

Article appearing in "Notas" section, under heading "Los libros."

220. Borges, Jorge Luis.

"Leyes de la narración policial." (In: *Hoy Argentina*, Año I, no. 2, pp. 48-49. Buenos Aires, April 1933).

221. Borges, Jorge Luis.

Livre de préfaces. Traduit de l'espagnol par Françoise-Marie Rosset. Suivi de: "Essai d'autobiographie." Traduit de l'anglais par Michel Seymour Tripier. [Paris:] Gallimard, [1980].
[1-8] 9-289 [290-296] p. 20.5 cm.
(Du monde entier.)

French translations of: *Prólogos con un prólogo de prólogos* and *An Autobiographical Essay.*

222. Borges, Jorge Luis.

Macedonio Fernández. Buenos Aires: Ediciones Culturales Argentinas. Ministerio de Educación y Justicia. Dirección General de Cultura, [1961].
[1-6] 7-154 [155-156] p. 20 cm.
(Biblioteca del sesquicentenario. Colección antologías.)

BECCO 189

223. Borges, Jorge Luis.

"Macedonio Fernández." (In: *Cahiers de L'Herne*, no. 4, pp. 65-70. Paris, 1964).

Appears in "Textes inédits" section. 3 copies.

224. Borges, Jorge Luis.

"1810-1960." (In: *Sur*, no. 267, pp. [1]-2. Buenos Aires, November-December 1960).

225. Borges, Jorge Luis.

"Modos de G. K. Chesterton." (In: *Sur*, Año VI, no. 22, pp. [47]-53. Buenos Aires, July 1936).

226. Borges, Jorge Luis.

"La muerte de Leopoldo Lugones." (In: *Cuadernos*, no. 76, pp. 17-19. Paris, September 1963).

2 copies.

227. Borges, Jorge Luis.

"El nacionalismo y Tagore." (In: *Sur*, no. 270, pp. [60]-61. Buenos Aires, May-June 1961).

On p. 1 of this issue the number and date are given as "Número 269, marzo-abril de 1961."

228. Borges, Jorge Luis.

"La nadería de la personalidad." (In: *Proa*, Año I, no. 1, [pp. 2-3]. Buenos Aires, August 1922).

229. Borges, Jorge Luis.

"Nota sobre (hacia) Bernard Shaw." (In: *Sur*, no. 200, pp. [1]-4. Buenos Aires, June 1951).

230. Borges, Jorge Luis.

"Nota sobre Chesterton." (In: *Los anales de Buenos Aires*, Año II, nos. 20-22, pp. 49-52. Buenos Aires, October-December 1947).

2 copies.

231. Borges, Jorge Luis.

"Nota sobre el Ulises en español." (In: *Los anales de Buenos Aires*, Año I, no. 1, p. 49. Buenos Aires, January 1946).

2 copies.

232. Borges, Jorge Luis.

"Nota sobre el ultraísmo." (In: *Testigo*, no. 2, pp. 8-9. Buenos Aires, April-June 1966).

233. Borges, Jorge Luis.

"Nota sobre Walt Whitman." (In: *Los anales de Buenos Aires*, Año II, no. 13, pp. 41-45. Buenos Aires, March 1947).

2 copies.

234. Borges, Jorge Luis.

Novas inquirições. [Lisboa:] Editorial Querco, [1983].
[1-8] 9-227 [228] p. 21 cm.
(Horizonte, 1.)

Portuguese translation of: *Otras inquisiciones*.

235. Borges, Jorge Luis.

Nove ensaios dantescos. [Lisboa:] Editorial Presença, [1984].
[1-6] 7-94 [95-96] p. 18 cm.
(Biblioteca universal Presença, 17.)

Portuguese translation of: *Nueve ensayos dantescos.*

236. Borges, Jorge Luis.

"Nuestras imposibilidades." (In: *Sur*, Año I, no. 4, pp. [131]-134. Buenos Aires, Spring 1931).

Article appearing in "Notas" section.

237. Borges, Jorge Luis.

"Nuestro pobre individualismo." (In: *Sur*, Año XV, no. 141, pp. [82]-84. Buenos Aires, July 1946).

Article appearing in "Notas" section.

238. Borges, Jorge Luis.

Nueve ensayos dantescos. Introducción de Marcos Ricardo Barnatán. Presentación por Joaquín Arce. Madrid: Espasa-Calpe, S.A., 1982.
[1-11] 12-161 [162-176] p. 17 cm.
(Selecciones Austral, 102.)

239. Borges, Jorge Luis.

"Nydia Lamarque. Telarañas, 1925." (In: *Proa*, Año II, no. 14, p. 50. Buenos Aires, December 1925).

240. Borges, Jorge Luis.

"Olaf Stapledon: Philosophy and Living." (In: *Sur*, Año X, no. 64, p. 85. Buenos Aires, January 1940).

Article appearing in "Notas" section, under heading "Los libros."

241. Borges, Jorge Luis.

"Omar Jaiyam y Fitzgerald." (In: *Proa*, Año II, no. 6, pp. 69-70. Buenos Aires, January 1925).

242. Borges, Jorge Luis.

Other Inquisitions, 1937-1952. Translated by Ruth L. C. Simms. Introduction by James E. Irby. New York: Washington Square Press, Inc., [1966].
[i-vi] vii-xiv [xv-xviii], 1-221 [222] p. 17.5 cm.

First printing. Gift of C. Alan Hutchinson. English translation of: *Otras inquisiciones.*

BECCO 274

243. Borges, Jorge Luis.

Otras inquisiciones. [Buenos Aires:] Emecé Editores, [1960].
[1-8] 9-259 [260-264] p. 18.5 cm.
(Obras completas, 8.)

First edition in this series.

BECCO 71

244. Borges, Jorge Luis.

Otras inquisiciones (1937-1952). Buenos Aires: Sur S. R. L., [1952].
[3-8] 9-226 [227-228] p. 20.5 cm.

First edition. Lacks first leaf [pp. 1-2]. Special binding.

BECCO 70

245. Borges, Jorge Luis.

Otras inquisiciones (1937-1952). Buenos Aires: Sur S. R. L., [1952].
[1-8] 9-226 [227-228] p. 20.5 cm.

Second edition.

BECCO 70

246. Borges, Jorge Luis.

Otras inquisiciones. [Buenos Aires:] Emecé Editores, [1966, c. 1960].
[1-8] 9-263 [264-268] p. 18.5 cm.
(Obras completas, 8.)

Third printing.

[BECCO 72]

247. Borges, Jorge Luis.

Otras inquisiciones. [Buenos Aires:] Emecé Editores, [1976, c. 1960].
[1-8] 9-247 [248-256] p. 18.5 cm.
(Obras completas.)

Tenth printing.

[BECCO 72]

248. Borges, Jorge Luis.

"Página sobre Shakespeare." (In: *Sur*, no. 289-290, pp. [28]-29. Buenos Aires, July-October 1964).

249. Borges, Jorge Luis.

"Palabras pronunciadas por Jorge Luis Borges en la comida que le ofrecieron los escritores." (In: *Sur*, Año XV, no. 142, pp. 114-115. Buenos Aires, August 1946).

Article appearing in "Notas" section. 2 copies.

250. Borges, Jorge Luis.

"Para el advenimiento de Pirandello." (In: *Síntesis*, Año I, no. 2, p. 116. Buenos Aires, July 1927).

Article appearing in "Notas" section.

251. Borges, Jorge Luis.

"Parábola de Cervantes y del *Quijote*." (In: *Sur*, no. 233, p. 3. Buenos Aires, March-April 1955).

2 copies.

252. Borges, Jorge Luis.

"La paradoja de Apollinaire." (In: *Los anales de Buenos Aires*, Año I, no. 8, pp. 48-51. Buenos Aires, August 1946).

2 copies.

253. Borges, Jorge Luis.

"Pascal: '*Pensées*'." (In: *Sur*, Año XVI, no. 157, pp. [97]-99. Buenos Aires, November 1947).

Article appearing in "Notas" section, under heading "Libros."

254. Borges, Jorge Luis.

"Paul Groussac." (In: *La revue argentine*, 2e Année, no. 13, pp. [33]-36. Paris, December 1935-January 1936).

255. Borges, Jorge Luis.

"La personalidad y el Buddha." (In: *Sur*, Año XIX, no. 192-194, pp. 31-34. Buenos Aires, October-December 1950).

Photograph of Jorge Luis Borges, Norah Borges, Victoria Ocampo, and other literary figures, facing p. 16. 2 copies.

256. Borges, Jorge Luis.

"La poesía gauchesca." (In: *Ars, revista de arte*, Año XX, no. 89, pp. [27-41]. Buenos Aires, 1960).

257. Borges, Jorge Luis.

La poesía gauchesca. [Buenos Aires: Centro de Estudios Brasileiros, 1961].
[1-4] 5-18 [19-20] p. 23 cm.
(Publicaçoes, 1.)

Series number given in volume; series title not shown in volume. 2 copies.

BECCO 74

258. Borges, Jorge Luis.

"Poetas de Buenos Aires." (In: *Testigo*, no. 1, pp. 3-13. Buenos Aires, January-March 1966).

259. Borges, Jorge Luis.

"Pornographie et censure." (In: *Cahiers de L'Herne*, no. 4, p. 96. Paris, 1964).

Appears in "Textes inédits" section. 3 copies.

260. Borges, Jorge Luis.

"Préface à la métamorphose." (In: *Obliques*, no. 3, pp. 15-16. Les Pilles, 1978).

Special issue on Kafka.

261. Borges, Jorge Luis.

"El primer Wells." (In: *Los anales de Buenos Aires*, Año I, no. 9, pp. 20-22. Buenos Aires, September 1946).

2 copies.

262. Borges, Jorge Luis.

"Primitivo R. Sanjurjo." (In: *Síntesis*, Año I, no. 2, p. 115. Buenos Aires, July 1927).

Article appearing in "Notas" section.

263. Borges, Jorge Luis.

Prólogos, con un prólogo de prólogos. Buenos Aires: Torres Agüero Editor, 1975.
[1-7] 8-174 [175-176] p. 20 cm.

First edition. 2 copies.

264. Borges, Jorge Luis.

"Prologue à Edward Gibbon pages d'histoire et d'autobiographie." (In: *Cahiers de L'Herne*, no. 4, pp. 83-84. Paris, 1964).

Appears in "Textes inédits" section. 3 copies.

265. Borges, Jorge Luis.

"'Psico-zoología pintoresca,' Domingo Sasso. Buenos Aires, 1927." (In: *Síntesis*, Año I, no. 3, pp. 123-124. Buenos Aires, August 1927).

Article appearing in "Bibliografía" section.

266. Borges, Jorge Luis.

"Los romances de Fernán Silva Valdés." (In: *Sur*, Año IX, no. 54, pp. 70-72. Buenos Aires, March 1939).

Article appearing in "Notas" section, under heading "Los libros."

267. Borges, Jorge Luis.

"Séneca en las orillas." (In: *Síntesis*, Año II, no. 19, pp. 29-32. Buenos Aires, December 1928).

Borges was a member of the editorial board of *Síntesis*. This article was republished in the first issue of *Sur* nearly three years later.

268. Borges, Jorge Luis.

"Séneca en las orillas." (In: *Sur*, Año I, no. 1, pp. 174-179. Buenos Aires, Summer 1931).

Number 83 of 100 copies. First issue of the magazine *Sur*. This article originally appeared in the journal *Síntesis* in December 1928.

269. Borges, Jorge Luis.

Sette notte. Milano: Feltrinelli Editore, [1983].
[1-6] 7-142 [143-144] p. 22 cm.
(Saggi e biografie, 520.)

First edition. Italian translation of: *Siete noches.*

270. Borges, Jorge Luis.

"Shakespeare y las unidades." (In: *Cuadernos*, no. 87, p. 2. Paris, August 1964).

271. Borges, Jorge Luis.

Siete noches. Epílogo de Roy Bartholomew.
México: Fondo de Cultura Económica, [1980].
[1-8] 9-173 [174-176] p. 21 cm.
(Colección tierra firme.)

First edition. 1 unnumbered leaf with black-and-white photograph of Borges facing title page.

272. Borges, Jorge Luis.

"Silvina Ocampo: 'Enumeración de la patria'." (In: *Sur*, Año XII, no. 101, pp. [64]-67. Buenos Aires, February 1943).

Article appearing in "Notas" section, under heading "Los libros."

273. Borges, Jorge Luis.

"Sir Thomas Browne." (In: *Proa*, Año II, no. 7, pp. 3-8. Buenos Aires, February 1925).

274. Borges, Jorge Luis.

"Sobre Don Segundo Sombra." (In: *Sur*, no. 217-218, pp. 9-11. Buenos Aires, November-December 1952).

2 copies.

275. Borges, Jorge Luis.

"Sobre los clásicos." (In: *Sur*, no. 298-299, pp. [3]-4. Buenos Aires, January-April 1966).

276. Borges, Jorge Luis.

"Sobre Oscar Wilde." (In: *Los anales de Buenos Aires*, Año I, no. 11, pp. 44-46. Buenos Aires, December 1946).

2 copies.

277. Borges, Jorge Luis.

"Spinoza, une figure pathétique." (In: *Europe*, no. 637, pp. [73]-76. Paris, May 1982).

278. Borges, Jorge Luis.

"Stories of Horsemen: The Gaucho and the City." (In: *The New Republic*, Issue 3514, pp. 6-7, 9. Washington, D. C., 19 May 1982).

Gift of James M. Campbell.

279. Borges, Jorge Luis.

"Le Sud." (In: *Cahiers de L'Herne*, no. 4, pp. 61-64. Paris, 1964).

Appears in "Textes inédits" section. 3 copies.

280. Borges, Jorge Luis.

"Swinburne." (In: *Sur*, Año VII, no. 33, pp. 93-94. Buenos Aires, June 1937).

Article appearing in "Notas" section, under heading "Centenarios." 2 copies.

281. Borges, Jorge Luis.

El tamaño de mi esperanza. Buenos Aires: Editorial Proa, 1926.
[1-4] 5-153 [154-160] p. 19.5 cm.

First and only edition. Borges never allowed this work to be republished. 2 copies. One copy contains author's autograph inscription: "A Lysandro Z. D. Galtier,/con la cordialidá de/Jorge Luis Borges." This copy also contains two ownership stamps of Galtier. Minor handwritten textual revisions. Also present is the owner's autograph: "Lysandro Z. D. Galtier/Bs.As." and various inscriptions relating to Galtier's family on final (volume) leaf. This copy bound with first editions of *Fervor de Buenos Aires* and *Inquisiciones* (external spine height, 18.5 cm.). Second copy is as issued originally.

BECCO 51

282. Borges, Jorge Luis.

"El tiempo y J. W. Dunne." (In: *Sur*, Año IX, no. 72, pp. 74-77. Buenos Aires, September 1940).

Article appearing in "Notas" section. 2 copies.

283. Borges, Jorge Luis.

"La Tierra Cárdena." (In: *Proa*, Año II, no. 13, pp. 52-54. Buenos Aires, November 1925).

284. Borges, Jorge Luis.

"Torres Villarroel." (In: *Proa*, Año I, no. 4, pp. 51-55. Buenos Aires, November 1924).

285. Borges, Jorge Luis.

"El Ulises de Joyce." (In: *Proa*, Año II, no. 6, pp. 3-6. Buenos Aires, January 1925).

286. Borges, Jorge Luis.

"L'Ulysse de Joyce." (In: *Europe*, no. 637, pp. [69]-72. Paris, May 1982).

287. Borges, Jorge Luis.

"Valéry como símbolo." (In: *Sur*, Año XIV, no. 132, pp. [30]-32. Buenos Aires, October 1945).

288. Borges, Jorge Luis.

"Verdes paredes, film." (In: *Sur*, Año VII, no. 37, pp. 87-88. Buenos Aires, October 1937).

Article appearing in "Cine" section.

289. Borges, Jorge Luis.

"El verdugo piadoso." (In: *Sur*, Año XVI, no. 163, pp. [9]-12. Buenos Aires, May 1948).

290. Borges, Jorge Luis.

"Walt Whitman: 'Canto a mí mismo'." (In: *Sur*, Año XII, no. 88, pp. 68-70. Buenos Aires, January 1942).

Article appearing in "Notas" section, under heading "Los libros."

291. Borges, Jorge Luis.

"Wells, previsor." (In: *Sur*, Año VI, no. 26, pp. [125]-126. Buenos Aires, November 1936).

Article appearing in "Cine" section.

292. Borges, Jorge Luis.

Zeven avonden. Vertaling Barber van de Pol. Amsterdam: Uitgeverij De Bezige Bij, 1983. [1-6] 7-186 [187-192] p. 20 cm. (BB literair.)

Dutch translation of: *Siete noches.*

IV. SHORT STORIES

293. Borges, Jorge Luis.

"Abenjacán el Bojarí, muerto en su laberinto." (In: *Sur*, no. 202, pp. [1]-8. Buenos Aires, August 1951).

2 copies.

294. Borges, Jorge Luis.

El aleph. Buenos Aires: Editorial Losada, S. A., [1949].
[1-6] 7-146 [147-152] p. 20.5 cm.
(Prosistas de España y América.)

First edition. 2 copies. With page from the journal *Caras y caretas* containing Borges' poem "Soneto para un tango en la nochecita" laid in one copy.

BECCO 37

295. Borges, Jorge Luis.

El aleph. Buenos Aires: Editorial Losada, S. A., [1952].
[1-6] 7-157 [158-160] p. 20 cm.
(Novelistas de España y América.)

Second edition. 2 copies.

BECCO 38

296. Borges, Jorge Luis.

El aleph. Buenos Aires-Barcelona: Emecé Editores, [1968].
[1-6] 7-198 [199-208] p. 17 cm.
(Colección Piragua, 55.)

Ninth edition.

[BECCO 43]

297. Borges, Jorge Luis.

El aleph. Madrid: Alianza Editorial/ Buenos Aires: Emecé Editores, [1971].
[1-6] 7-184 p. 18 cm.
(El libro de bolsillo. 309. Sección: literatura.)

BECCO 45

298. Borges, Jorge Luis.

L'aleph. Traduit de l'espagnol par Roger Caillois et Réné L. F. Durand. [Paris:] Gallimard, [1976, c. 1967].
[1-7] 8-218 [219-224] p. 18.5 cm.
(Du monde entier.)

French translation of: *El aleph.*

[BECCO 259]

299. Borges, Jorge Luis.

L'aleph. Traduit de l'espagnol par Roger Caillois et Réné L. F. Durand. [Paris:] Gallimard, [1977, c. 1967].
[1-7] 8-218 [219-224] p. 19 cm.
(L'imaginaire, 13.)

French translation of: *El aleph.*

BECCO 258

300. Borges, Jorge Luis.

The Aleph and Other Stories, 1933-1969. Together with Commentaries and an Autobiographical Essay. Edited and translated by Norman Thomas di Giovanni in collaboration with the author. New York: E. P. Dutton & Co., Inc., 1970.
[1-6] 7-286 [287-288] p. 24 cm.

First edition. English translation of: *El aleph,* with additional "Autobiographical Essay" appended.

This latter piece was an original text in English by Borges. Gift of Joan St. C. Crane.

BECCO 281

301. Borges, Jorge Luis.

The Aleph and Other Stories, 1933-1969. Together with Commentaries and an Autobiographical Essay. Edited and translated by Norman Thomas di Giovanni in collaboration with the author. London: Jonathan Cape, [1971].
[1-14] 15-286 [287-288] p. 21.5 cm.

First British edition. English translation of: *El aleph.* Proof state, in wrappers. Publisher's notes for dust jacket pasted on front cover.

BECCO 282

302. Borges, Jorge Luis.

De aleph en andere verhalen. Vertaling Annie Sillevis. Amsterdam: Uitgeverij De Bezige Bij, 1976.
[1-5] 6-169 [170-176] p. 20 cm.
(BB literair.)

Third edition. Dutch translations of: *El aleph* and *Ficciones.*

[BECCO 265]

303. Borges, Jorge Luis.

"La biblioteca total." (In: *Sur*, Año IX, no. 59, pp. [13]-16. Buenos Aires, August 1939).

304. Borges, Jorge Luis.

Die bibliothek von Babel. Stuttgart: Philipp Reclam, [1974].

[1-2] 3-83 [84-88] p. 15 cm.
(Universal-Bibliothek, 9497.)

German translation of: *La biblioteca de Babel.*

305. Borges, Jorge Luis.

La bibliothèque de Babel. Montanthiaume: Raymond Gid, [1963].
[i-iv], [1-10] 11-30 [31-44] p. 27 cm.

Copy number 88 of 100. Signed by the artist-printer Raymond Gid.

BECCO 252

306. Borges, Jorge Luis.

"Biografía de Tadeo Isidoro Cruz (1829-1874)." (In: *Sur*, Año XIV, no. 122, pp. [7]-10. Buenos Aires, December 1944).

307. Borges, Jorge Luis.

Het boek van zand. Vertaling Mariolein Sabarte Belacortu. Amsterdam: De Bezige Bij, 1977.
[1-8] 9-159 [160] p. 20.5 cm.
(BB literair.)

Dutch translation of: *El libro de arena.*

308. Borges, Jorge Luis.

The Book of Sand. Translated by Norman Thomas di Giovanni. New York: E. P. Dutton, [1977].
[i-ii], [1-6] 7-125 [126] p. 24 cm.

English translation of: *El libro de arena.* First edition.

309. Borges, Jorge Luis.

"La busca de Averroes." (In: *Sur*, Año XVI, no. 152, pp. [36]-45. Buenos Aires, June 1947).

310. Borges, Jorge Luis.

"La casa de Asterión." (In: *Los anales de Buenos Aires*, Año II, nos. 15-16, pp. 47-48. Buenos Aires, May-June 1947).

2 copies.

311. Borges, Jorge Luis.

El congreso. Buenos Aires: El Archibrazo Editor, 1971.
[1-10] 11-56 [57-64] p. 27.5 cm.
(Cuadernos del Archibrazo Editor.)

First edition. 2 copies. One copy is number 456 of 3,000 copies. Second copy is number 2,299.

BECCO 49

312. Borges, Jorge Luis.

The Congress. Translated by Norman Thomas di Giovanni in collaboration with the author. London: Enitharmon Press, 1974.
[i-viii], 1-7 [8-24] p. 25 cm.

One of 50 copies, this is the "Author's copy," without the signatures of author and translator. English translation of: *El congreso*. Includes frontispiece portrait of Borges by Hugo Manning.

313. Borges, Jorge Luis.

The Congress of the World. With miniatures of tantric cosmology introduced by Alain Daniélon. [Milano:] Franco Maria Ricci, [1981].

[1-14] 15-144 [145-152] p. 35.5 cm.
(The Signs of Man, 8.)

English translation of: *El congreso.* Includes an interview of Borges by María Esther Vásquez, as well as a chronology of his life and a bibliography of his works. Copy number 1,062 of 4,000. Signed by the publisher. Boxed.

314. Borges, Jorge Luis.

Cuentos. Selección de Carlos Mastronardi. [Buenos Aires:] Centro Editor de América Latina, [1968].
[1-4] 5-111 [112] p. 18 cm.
(Capítulo. Biblioteca argentina fundamental, 48.)

2 copies.

BECCO 85

315. Borges, Jorge Luis.

Cuentos; antología. Selección por Carlos Mastronardi. Prólogo por la profesora Noemí Ulla. [Buenos Aires:] Centro Editor de América Latina, [1981].
[1 unnumbered leaf], [1-4], i-vii [viii], 5-111 [112-118] p. 18 cm.
(Capítulo. Biblioteca argentina fundamental, 79.)

[BECCO 85]

316. Borges, Jorge Luis.

"The Cypress Leaves." (In: *New England Review*, Vol. II, no. 1, pp. 1-2. Hanover, N.H., Autumn 1979).

Short story written for María Kodama, and translated into English by Alastair Reid.

317. Borges, Jorge Luis.

David Brodies Bericht. Erzählungen. Aus dem Spanischen von Curt Meyer-Clason. [München:] Carl Hanser Verlag, [1972].
[1-6] 7-97 [98-100] p. 18.5 cm.
(Reihe Hanser, 86).

German translation of: *El informe de Brodie.*

BECCO 246

318. Borges, Jorge Luis.

David Brodies Rapport. [Uppsala:] Brombergs, [1978].
[1-6] 7-150 [151-152] p. 20 cm.

Swedish translation of: *El informe de Brodie.*

319. Borges, Jorge Luis.

"Deutsches requiem." (In: *Sur*, Año XV, no. 136, pp. [7]-14. Buenos Aires, February 1946).

2 copies.

320. Borges, Jorge Luis.

Doctor Brodie's Report. Translation by Norman Thomas di Giovanni in collaboration with the author. New York: E. P. Dutton & Co., Inc., 1972.
[1-6] 7-128 p. 24 cm.

First edition. English translation of: *El informe de Brodie.* Gift of Joan St. C. Crane.

BECCO 285

321. Borges, Jorge Luis.

"Emma Zunz." (In: *Sur*, Año XVI, no. 167, pp. [14]-19. Buenos Aires, September 1948).

322. Borges, Jorge Luis.

"La escritura del Dios." (In: *Sur*, Año XVII, no. 172, pp. [7]-12. Buenos Aires, February 1949).

2 copies.

323. Borges, Jorge Luis.

"Los espejos velados." (In: *Destiempo*, Año I, no. 1, p. 3. Buenos Aires, October 1936).

324. Borges, Jorge Luis.

El evangelio según Marcos. Buenos Aires: [Francisco A. Colombo, 1971].
12 unnumbered leaves [pp. 1-24]. 33.5 cm.

Copy number 41 of 41 signed copies, this one printed for Norman Thomas di Giovanni.

BECCO 154

325. Borges, Jorge Luis.

Ficciones. [Buenos Aires:] Emecé Editores, S. A., [1956].
[1-10] 11-197 [198-200] p. 19 cm.
(Obras completas, 5.)

BECCO 31

326. Borges, Jorge Luis.

Ficciones. Buenos Aires-Barcelona: Emecé Editores, [1966].
[1-10] 11-186 [187-196] p. 17 cm.
(Colección piragua, 104.)

Sixth edition.

BECCO 33

327. Borges, Jorge Luis.

Ficciones. [Buenos Aires:] Emecé Editores, [1966, c. 1956].
[1-10] 11-197 [198-200] p. 19 cm.
(Obras completas, 5.)

Seventh printing.

[BECCO 32]

328. Borges, Jorge Luis.

Ficciones. Buenos Aires-Barcelona: Emecé Editores, [1968].
[1-10] 11-186 [187-196] p. 17 cm.
(Colección piragua, 104.)

Ninth edition.

[BECCO 32]

329. Borges, Jorge Luis.

Ficciones. [Buenos Aires:] Emecé Editores, [1969].
[1-10] 11-197 [198-200] p. 18.5 cm.
(Obras completas.)

Eleventh printing.

[BECCO 32]

330. Borges, Jorge Luis.

Ficciones. Madrid: Alianza Editorial/ Buenos Aires: Emecé Editores, [1971, c. 1956].
[1-10] 11-206 [207-212] p. 18 cm.
(El libro de bolsillo, 320; Sección literatura.)

BECCO 34

331. Borges, Jorge Luis.

Ficciones. Madrid-México-Buenos Aires: Aguilar, [1981].
[1-8] 9-387 [388-392] p. 8 cm.
(Colección crisol, 44.) (Serie especial.)

First edition in this series.

332. Borges, Jorge Luis.

Ficciones. [New York: The Limited Editions Club, 1984].
[2 unnumbered leaves], [i-xiv] xv-xxxii, [1-6] 7-306 [307-312] p. 21 cm.

Copy number 1,484 of 1,500. Signed by the artist, Sol Lewitt.

English translation of: *Ficciones.*

333. Borges, Jorge Luis.

Ficciones (1935-1944). Buenos Aires: Sur, [1944].
[1-8] 9-203 [204] p. 21 cm.

First edition. Contains frontispiece portrait of Borges on unnumbered leaf. With author's autograph: "Jorge Luis Borges."

BECCO 30

334. Borges, Jorge Luis.

Fictions. Edited and with an introduction by Anthony Kerrigan. London: John Calder, [1965].
[1-9] 10-159 [160] p. 18 cm.
(A Jupiter book, J-7.)

English translation of: *Ficciones.*

BECCO 269

335. Borges, Jorge Luis.

Fictions. Traduit de l'espagnol par P. Verdevoye et Ibarra. Edition revue et augmentée. [Paris:] Gallimard, [1968, c. 1957].
[1-7] 8-198 [199-200] p. 18.5 cm.
(Du monde entier.)

French translation of: *Ficciones.*

[BECCO 248]

336. Borges, Jorge Luis.

Fictions. Traduit de l'espagnol par P. Verdevoye et Ibarra. Edition revue et augmentée. [Paris:] Gallimard, [1977, c. 1957].
[1-7] 8-198 [199-200] p. 18.5 cm.

French translation of: *Ficciones.*

[BECCO 248]

337. Borges, Jorge Luis.

Fictions. Préface d'Ibarra. Traduit de l'espagnol par P. Verdevoye et Ibarra. Edition revue et augmentée. [Paris:] Gallimard, [1978, c. 1957].
[1-7] 8-186 [187-192] p. 18 cm.
(Collection folio, 614.)

French translation of: *Ficciones.*

[BECCO 248]

338. Borges, Jorge Luis.

"El fin." (In: *Ficción*, no. 24-25, pp. [199]-201. Buenos Aires, March-June 1960).

339. Borges, Jorge Luis.

Finzioni. La biblioteca di Babele. Traduzione di Franco Lucentini. [Torino:] Einaudi, [1978]. [i-iv], [1-5] 6-146 [147-156] p. 19.5 cm. (Nuovi coralli, 214.)

Italian translation of: *Ficciones.*

[BECCO 289]

340. Borges, Jorge Luis.

Gavornasnatt. Översättning: Lasse Söderberg. [Uppsala:] Brombergs, [1979]. [1-8] 9-175 [176] p. 20 cm.

Swedish translation of: *El libro de arena.*

341. Borges, Jorge Luis.

"El hacedor." (In: *La biblioteca*, Segunda Epoca, Vol. IX, no. 3, pp. 129-130. Buenos Aires, 1958).

2 copies.

342. Borges, Jorge Luis.

Histoire de l'infamie. Histoire de l'éternité. Traductions par Roger Caillois et Laure Guille. [Paris: Union Générale d'Editions, 1964, c. 1951].

[1-7] 8-310 [311-320] p. 18 cm.
(Le monde en 10/18, 184-185.)

French translations of: *Historia universal de la infamia* and *Historia de la eternidad.*

[BECCO 251]

343. Borges, Jorge Luis.

Histoire de l'infamie. Histoire de l'éternité.
Traductions par Roger Caillois et Laure Guille.
[Paris: Union Générale d'Editions, 1975, c. 1951].
[1-7] 8-310 [311-320] p. 17.5 cm.
(Collection 10/18, 184.)

French translations of: *Historia universal de la infamia* and *Historia de la eternidad.*

[BECCO 251]

344. Borges, Jorge Luis.

"Historia del guerrero y de la cautiva." (In: *Sur*, Año XVII, no. 175, pp. [40]-43. Buenos Aires, May 1949).

345. Borges, Jorge Luis.

História universal da infâmia. Tradução de José Beuto. [Lisboa:] Assírio e Alvim, [1982].
[1-6] 7-117 [118-120] p. 18.5 cm.
(Gato maltês, 4.)

Portuguese translation of: *Historia universal de la infamia.*

346. Borges, Jorge Luis.

Historia universal de la infamia. Buenos Aires: [Editorial Tor,] 1935.
[1-4] 5-139 [140-144] p. 19 cm.

(Colección megáfono, 3.)

First edition. 2 copies. One copy contains autograph inscription by Borges: "A Paco Luis, dedico estos breves juegos/visuales con el anacronismo y la muerte./Muy cordialmente Georgie." A second copy has a special binding.

BECCO 25

347. Borges, Jorge Luis.

Historia universal de la infamia. [Buenos Aires:] Emecé Editores, S. A., [1954].
[1-6] 7-137 [138-140] p. 18.5 cm.
(Obras completas, 3.)

Second edition. Back cover lacking.

BECCO 26

348. Borges, Jorge Luis.

Historia universal de la infamia. [Buenos Aires:] Emecé Editores, [1966, c. 1954].
[1-6] 7-137 [138-144] p. 19 cm.
(Obras completas, 3.)

Sixth printing.

[BECCO 27]

349. Borges, Jorge Luis.

Historia universal de la infamia. Buenos Aires-Barcelona: Emecé Editores, [1967].
[1-6] 7-149 [150-156] p. 17 cm.
(Colección piragua, 134.)

Seventh edition.

[BECCO 27]

350. Borges, Jorge Luis.

Historia universal de la infamia. Madrid: Alianza Editorial/ Buenos Aires: Emecé Editores, [1971].
[1-6] 7-139 [140] p. 18 cm.
(El libro de bolsillo, 353; Sección: literatura.)

BECCO 28

351. Borges, Jorge Luis.

El informe de Brodie. [Buenos Aires:] Emecé Editores, [1970].
[1-6] 7-153 [154-160] p. 18.5 cm.
(Obras completas.)

First printing (August 1970). 2 copies.

BECCO 47

352. Borges, Jorge Luis.

"Los inmortales." (In: *Los anales de Buenos Aires*, Año II, no. 12, pp. 29-39. Buenos Aires, February 1947).

2 copies.

353. Borges, Jorge Luis.

"Inscripciones." (In: *Destiempo*, Año I, no. 3, p. 3. Buenos Aires, December 1936).

354. Borges, Jorge Luis.

La intrusa. Ilustrado Emilio Centurión. [Buenos Aires: Francisco A. Colombo,] 1966.
8 unnumbered leaves [pp. 1-16]. 28 cm.

Number 27 of 52 copies. With an original drawing by Centurión on p. [7].

BECCO 149

355. Borges, Jorge Luis.

El jardín de senderos que se bifurcan. Buenos Aires: Sur, [1942].
[1-6] 7-124 [125-128] p. 21 cm.

First edition, bound copy.

BECCO 29

356. Borges, Jorge Luis.

Kongressen. Oversatt fra Spansk av Mona Lange. Forord av Olav Angell. [Oslo:] J. W. Cappelens Forlag, A. S., [1978].
[1-6] 7-130 [131-132] p. 20.5 cm.
(PAN-serien.)

Norwegian translation of: *El congress.*

357. Borges, Jorge Luis.

Laberintos. Prólogo de José Edmundo Clemente. [Buenos Aires: Editorial Joraci, 1977].
[1-4] 5-65 [66-80] p. 23 cm.

Includes 20 color reproductions of paintings by the Argentine painter Zdravko Ducmelic. 2 copies. One copy is number 339 of 3,000 copies. Second copy is number 669. Slipcased.

358. Borges, Jorge Luis.

Labyrinthe; Erzählungen. [München:] Deutscher Taschenbuch Verlag, [1969].
[1-6] 7-168 [169-176] p. 18 cm.
(Sonderreihe DTV, 6.)

Translations into German from *Ficciones* and *El aleph.*

[BECCO 236]

359. Borges, Jorge Luis.

El libro de arena. [Buenos Aires:] Emecé Editores, [1975].
[1-8] 9-181 [182-192] p. 18.5 cm.
(Obras completas.)

First edition. 2 copies.

360. Borges, Jorge Luis.

El libro de arena. Madrid: Alianza Editorial, [1980].
[1-6] 7-104 p. 18 cm.
(El libro de bolsillo; Sección: literatura, 662.)

Third edition.

361. Borges, Jorge Luis.

Libro delle visioni di Jorge Luis Borges. Saggio storico-critico sull'iconografia di Mariusz Karpowicz. [Milano:] Franco Maria Ricci, [1980].
[1-9] 10-144 [145-152] p. 35 cm.
(I segni dell'uomo, 26.)

Includes a prologue by Borges, as well as his "25 agosto 1983" in Italian translation. Copy no. two, 195 of 3,000. Signed by the publisher. Boxed.

362. Borges, Jorge Luis.

Il libro di sabbia. Traduzione di Livio Bacchi Wilcock. [Milan:] Rizzoli Editore, [1977].
[1-6] 7-160 [161-168] p. 22.5 cm.
(La Scala.)

Italian translation of: *El libro de arena.*

363. Borges, Jorge Luis.

Le livre de sable. Traduit de l'espagnol par Françoise-Marie Rosset. [Paris:] Gallimard, [1979, c. 1978].
[1-7] 8-146 [147-152] p. 18.5 cm.
(Du monde entier.)

French translation of: *El libro de arena.*

364. Borges, Jorge Luis.

O livro de areia. [Lisboa:] Editorial Estampa, [1981].
[1-4] 5-134 [135-136] p. 18.5 cm.
(Livro B, 39.)

Portuguese translation of: *El libro de arena.*

365. Borges, Jorge Luis.

"La lotería de Babilonia." (In: *Letras nacionales*, no. 15, pp. [78]-84. Bogotá, July-August 1967).

Gift of Donald McGrady.

366. Borges, Jorge Luis.

Il manoscritto di Brodie. Milano: Rizzoli Editore, 1984.
[1-8] 9-116 [117-120] p. 20 cm.
(La piccola scala Rizzoli.)

Italian translation of: *El informe de Brodie.*

367. Borges, Jorge Luis.

"El milagro secreto." (In: *Sur*, Año XII, no. 101, pp. [13]-20. Buenos Aires, February 1943).

368. Borges, Jorge Luis.

La muerte y la brújula. Buenos Aires: Emecé Editores, S. A., [1951].
[1-10] 11-149 [150-152] p. 18.5 cm.
(Novelistas argentinos contemporáneos.)

First edition. 2 copies.

BECCO 46

369. Borges, Jorge Luis.

La muerte y la brújula. Ilustrado por [Roberto] Páez. [Buenos Aires:] Centro Editor de América Latina, [1971].
10 unnumbered leaves [pp. 1-20]. 28 cm.

2 copies.

BECCO 36

370. Borges, Jorge Luis.

"El muerto." (In: *Sur*, Año XV, no. 145, pp. [42]-48. Buenos Aires, November 1946).

371. Borges, Jorge Luis.

"Mutaciones." (In: *Sur*, no. 228, p. [1], Buenos Aires, May-June 1954).

372. Borges, Jorge Luis.

Narraciones. Edición de Marcos Ricardo Barnatán. Madrid: Ediciones Cátedra, S. A., [1981]. [1-6] 7-251 [252-256] p. 18 cm. (Letras hispánicas, 123.)

Second edition.

373. Borges, Jorge Luis.

"Parábola del palacio." (In: *Sur*, no. 243, pp. [1]-2. Buenos Aires, November-December 1956).

2 copies.

374. Borges, Jorge Luis.

"Pedro Leandro Ipuche." (In: *Ficción*, no. 5, p. [66]. Buenos Aires, January-February 1957).

375. Borges, Jorge Luis.

"Pierre Menard, autor del *Quijote*." (In: *Sur*, Año IX, no. 56, pp. [7]-16. Buenos Aires, May 1939).

First appearance of an important title in the Borges canon.

376. Borges, Jorge Luis.

"Prosas." (In: *La biblioteca*, Segunda Epoca, Vol. IX, no. 1, pp. 116-118. Buenos Aires, 1957).

Includes "El cautivo," "El simulacro," "Borges y yo," and "Delia Elena San Marco."

377. Borges, Jorge Luis.

"Prosas." (In: *La biblioteca*, Segunda Epoca, Vol. IX, no. 2, pp. 44-47. Buenos Aires, 1957).

Includes "Diálogo de muertos," "La trama," and "Un problema."

378. Borges, Jorge Luis.

"Prosas: El testigo. Martín Fierro." (In: *Sur*, no. 247, pp. 16-17. Buenos Aires, July-August 1957).

379. Borges, Jorge Luis.

"El puñal." (In: *Ficción*, no. 18, p. [6]. Buenos Aires, March-April 1959).

380. Borges, Jorge Luis.

"Ragnarok." (In: *Sur*, no. 257, p. 50. Buenos Aires, March-April 1959).

381. Borges, Jorge Luis.

Le rapport de Brodie. Traduit de l'espagnol par Françoise-Marie Rosset. [Paris:] Gallimard, [1978, c. 1972].
[1-7] 8-138 [139-144] p. 18.5 cm.
(Du monde entier.)

French translation of: *El informe de Brodie*.

[BECCO 262]

382. Borges, Jorge Luis.

O relatório de Brodie. Tradução e prefácio de António Alçada Baptista. Amadora: Livraria Bertrand, [1981].

[1-9] 10-143 [144-148] p. 20 cm.
(Colecção autores universais.)

Second edition. Portuguese translation of: *El informe de Brodie.*

383. Borges, Jorge Luis.

Samtliche Erzählungen. Das aleph. Fictionen. Universalgeschichte der Niedertracht. [München:] Carl Hanser Verlag, [1970].
[1-6] 7-347 [348-352] p. 21 cm.
(Die Bücher der Neunzehn, 190.)

German translations of: *El aleph, Ficciones, Historia universal de la infamia.*

BECCO 244

384. Borges, Jorge Luis.

Das Sandbuch. Aus dem Spanischen von Dieter E. Zimmer. [München:] Carl Hanser Verlag, [1977].
[1-6] 7-118 [119-120] p. 18.5 cm.
(Reihe Hanser, 233.)

German translation of: *El libro de arena.*

385. Borges, Jorge Luis.

"La secta del fénix." (In: *Sur*, no. 215-216, pp. 13-15. Buenos Aires, September-October 1952).

386. Borges, Jorge Luis.

Storia universale dell'infamia. Introduzione di Carlo Fruttero e Franco Lucentini. Traduzione di Mario Pasi. [Milano:] Il Saggiatore, [1981, c. 1961].
[1-4] 5-106 [107-112] p. 19 cm.
(Le silerchie nuova serie, 6.)

Second edition. Italian translation of: *Historia universal de la infamia.*

[BECCO 292]

387. Borges, Jorge Luis.

"Los teólogos." (In: *Los anales de Buenos Aires,* Año II, no. 14, pp. 50-56. Buenos Aires, April 1947).

2 copies.

388. Borges, Jorge Luis.

"Tlön, Uqbar, Orbis Tertius." (In: *Sur,* Año X, no. 68, pp. [30]-46. Buenos Aires, May 1940).

389. Borges, Jorge Luis.

Tlön, Uqbar, Orbis Tertius. Translated by James E. Irby. Illustrated by Rikki. [Erin, Ontario:] The Porcupine's Quill, 1983.
[1-6] 7-22 [27 unnumbered leaves] p. 22 cm.

Includes folding map.

390. Borges, Jorge Luis.

"Tres versiones de Judas." (In: *Sur,* Año XIV, no. 118, pp. [7]-12. Buenos Aires, August 1944).

391. Borges, Jorge Luis.

A Universal History of Infamy. Translated by Norman Thomas di Giovanni. New York: E. P. Dutton & Co., Inc., 1972.
[1-10] 11-146 [147-152] p. 24 cm.

First edition. English translation of: *Historia universal de la infamia.* Gift of Joan St. C. Crane.

392. Borges, Jorge Luis.

A Universal History of Infamy. Translated by Norman Thomas di Giovanni. [London:] Allen Lane, [1973].
[1-10] 11-146 [147-152] p. 22.5 cm.

English translation of: *Historia universal de la infamia.*

393. Borges, Jorge Luis.

Veinticinco agosto 1983 y otros cuentos. Volumen en honor de J. L. Borges. [Madrid: Ediciones Siruela, S. A., 1983].
[1-10] 11-151 [152-160] p. 22.5 cm.
(La biblioteca de Babel, 2.) (Colección de lecturas fantásticas.)

394. Borges, Jorge Luis.

Venticinque agosto 1983 e altri racconti inediti di Jorge Luis Borges. Volume in onore di J. L. Borges nel suo 80 compleanno. [Milano: Franco Maria Ricci Editore, 1980].
[1-8] 9-147 [148-152] p. 22.5 cm.
(La biblioteca di Babele, 19.)

First edition. Italian translation of: *Veinticinco agosto 1983 y otros cuentos.* Includes four short stories, an interview of Borges by María Esther Vázquez, and a bibliography of Borges' principal works.

395. Borges, Jorge Luis.

Het verslag van Brodie. Vertaling Mariolein Sabarte Belacortu. Amsterdam: De Bezige Bij, 1979.
[1-6] 7-142 [143-144] p. 20 cm.

(BB literair.)

Dutch translation of: *El informe de Brodie.*

396. Borges, Jorge Luis.

Wereldschandkroniek. Amsterdam: Em. Querido's Uitgeverij B.V., 1978.
[1-8] 9-125 [126-128] p. 18.5 cm.
(Salamander, 455.)

Dutch translation of: *Historia universal de la infamia.*

397. Borges, Jorge Luis.

"El zahir." (In: *Los anales de Buenos Aires,* Año II, no. 17, pp. 30-37. Buenos Aires, July 1947).

2 copies.

398. Borges, Jorge Luis.

De Zahir. Vertaling Annie Sillevis. Amsterdam: De Bezige Bij, 1982.
[1-6] 7-203 [204-208] p. 20 cm.
(BB literair.)

Third edition. Dutch translations of: *El aleph* and *Ficciones.*

V. ANTHOLOGIES

399. *Adolfo de Obieta, Gabriel del Mazo, Federico Guillermo Pedrido, Enrique Villegas, Arturo Jauretche, Lily Laferrere, Miguel Shapire, Leopoldo Marechal, Manuel Peyrou, Francisco Luis Bernárdez, Jorge Luis Borges, Germán Leopoldo García hablan de Macedonio Fernández.* [Buenos Aires:] Carlos Pérez Editor, [1969, c. 1968].
[1-10] 11-127 [128] p. 19.5 cm.

Borges' essay appears on pp. 95-100. 2 copies.

400. *Anthology of Contemporary Latin-American Poetry.* Edited by Dudley Fitts. Norfolk, Conn.: A New Directions Book, 1947.
[2 unnumbered leaves], [i-vii] viii-xxi [xxii], [1] 2-677 [678] p. 22 cm.

First edition. Contains 10 poems by Borges and a brief biography. Gift of C. Jared Loewenstein.

401. *Antología de la poesía argentina moderna (1900-1925*). Con notas biográficas y bibliográficas. Ordenado por Julio Noé. Buenos Aires: Edición de "Nosotros," 1926.
[1-5] 6-603 [604-608] p. 21 cm.

Includes 6 poems by Borges and a brief biographical sketch.

402. *Apuntes, análisis y antología de literatura hispanoamericana.* Buenos Aires: Librería Huemul, [1972, c. 1968].
[1-6] 7-750 [751-752] p. 19.5 cm. At head of title: Instituto Cristo Redentor. Hermanas Franciscanas de Gante.

Third edition, second printing. Includes Borges' "La fundación mitológica de Buenos Aires."

403. Armani, Horacio.

Antología esencial de poesía argentina (1900-1980). [Buenos Aires:] Aguilar, [1982].
[1-8] 9-366 [367-368] p. 20 cm.

Second edition.

404. *Así escriben los argentinos.* Prólogo y notas: Haydée M. Jofré Barroso. Buenos Aires: Ediciones Orión, [1975].
[1-7] 8-279 [280-288] p. 18 cm.
(Colección así escriben.)

Includes Borges' *El otro duelo.*

405. Bartholomew, Roy

Cien poesías rioplatenses, 1800-1950. Antología. Ordenación, prólogo, notas sobre la poesía en el Río de la Plata y bio-bibliográficas de los poetas. Apéndice con los poemas de William Henry Hudson. [Buenos Aires:] Editorial Raigal, [1954].
[i-ix] x-liii [liv], [1-3] 4-398 [399-402] p. 24 cm.

2 copies. One copy contains editor's autograph inscription: "Al/insigne y noble poeta/Carlos Mastronardi,/con la profundísima/admiración y el/ respetuoso homenaje/de/Roy Bartholomew/ Buenos Aires, 1954./s/c. Luis Sáenz Peña 277, 4 c."

BECCO 437

406. *Boedo y Florida. J. L. Borges, R. González Tunón y otros.* Selección, prólogo y notas por la profesora María Raquel Llagostera. [Buenos Aires:] Centro Editor de América Latina, [1980].
[1-6], i-xi [xii], 7-175 [176-180] p. 18 cm.
(Capítulo. Biblioteca argentina fundamental, 64.)

407. *The Borzoi Anthology of Latin American Literature. Volume I: From the Time of Columbus to the Twentieth Century.* Edited by Emir Rodríguez Monegal with the assistance of Thomas Colchie. New York: Alfred A. Knopf, 1977.
[1 unnumbered leaf], [i-vi] vii-xv [xvi], [1] 2-493 [494] p. 23.5 cm.

First edition. Gift of C. Alan Hutchinson.

408. *The Borzoi Anthology of Latin American Literature. Volume II: The Twentieth Century from Borges and Paz to Guimarães Rosa and Donoso.* Edited by Emir Rodríguez Monegal with the assistance of Thomas Colchie. New York: Alfred A. Knopf, 1977.
[1 unnumbered leaf], [i-vi] vii-xiv, [495] 496-982 [983-990] p. 23.5 cm.

First edition. Gift of C. Alan Hutchinson.

409. Buenos Aires, Intendencia Municipal.

Homenaje a Buenos Aires en el cuarto centenario de su fundación. Ciclo de disertaciones histórico-literarias auspiciado por la Intendencia Municipal de la Ciudad de Buenos Aires. Buenos Aires: 1936.
[1-7] 8-556 [557-560] p. 22.5 cm. (without binding)

Borges' essay "Tareas y destino de Buenos Aires" appears in this work. One copy lacks pp. [1-2]. Copy number 1,142. Second copy is number 1,572. 2 copies, with differing binding styles.

410. *Cuentistas y pintores. Juan Carlos Dávalos, Leonidas Barletta, Mateo Booz, Arturo Cancela, Jorge Luis Borges, Roberto Arlt, Horacio Quiroga, Benito Lynch, Roberto J. Payró, Ricardo Güiraldes, Antonio Berni, Juan Batlle Planas, Juan C. Castagnino, Luis Seoane, Héctor Basaldúa, Demetrio Urruchúa, Carlos Alonso, Raúl Soldi, Enrique Policastro, Raúl Russo.* [Buenos Aires: Editorial Universitaria de Buenos Aires, 1963].
[1-6] 7-76 [77-80] p. 39 cm.

(Arte para todos. Cuentistas y pintores de América. Argentina.)

Contains Borges' "Hombre de la esquina rosada."

411. *El cuento argentino contemporáneo. Borges, Cortázar, S. Ocampo, Kordon, Moyano, Costantini, Conti, Walsh, Saer, J. J. Hernández, Rozenmacher, Castillo.* Selección y notas: Beatriz Sarlo. [Buenos Aires:] Centro Editor de América Latina, [1978, c. 1976].
[1-6] 7-154 [155-160] p. 18.5 cm.
(Biblioteca total, 7.) (Panoramas de la literatura, II.)

412. *El cuento argentino contemporáneo. J. L. Borges. J. Cortázar. S. Ocampo. B. Kordon. D. Moyano. J. Costantini. H. Conti. R. Walsh. J. J. Saer. J. J. Hernández. G. Rozenmacher y A. Castillo.* Selección y notas: Beatriz Sarlo. [Buenos Aires:] Centro Editor de América Latina, [1977, c. 1976].
[1-6] 7-154 [155-160] p. 18.5 cm.
(Biblioteca total, 7.) (Panoramas de la literatura, II.)

413. *El cuento argentino, 1930-1959. Antología. R. Arlt, J. L. Borges y otros.* Selección y prólogo por el profesor Eduardo Romano. Notas por la profesora Marta Bustos. [Buenos Aires:] Centro Editor de América Latina, [1981].
[1-6], i-viii, 7-183 [184] p. 18 cm.
(Capítulo. Biblioteca argentina fundamental, 83.)

414. *Cuentos argentinos de misterio.* Edited by E. Dale Carte, Jr., Joe Bas. New York: Irvington Publishers, Inc., [1968].
[1 unnumbered leaf], [i-iv] v-vii [viii], [1-2] 3-112 [113-118] p. 21 cm.

Contains: "La espera" and "Emma Zunz" by Borges, pp. 61-71. Text edition.

415. *Cuentos de dos orillas. Roberto Arlt. Mario Benedetti. Adolfo Bioy Casares. Jorge Luis Borges. Julio Cortázar. Felisberto Hernández. Carlos Martínez Moreno. Silvina Ocampo. Juan Carlos Onetti. Horacio Quiroga.* [Buenos Aires:] Centro Editor de América Latina, [1971].
[1-6] 7-150 [151-160] p. 17.5 cm.
(Biblioteca fundamental del hombre moderno, 4.)

Includes Borges' "Funes el memorioso."

416. *Cuentos fantásticos argentinos.* Selección de Nicolás Cócaro. Buenos Aires: Emecé Editores, [1960].
[1-10] 11-226 [227-228] p. 19 cm.
(Selección Emecé de obras contemporáneas.)

Includes Borges' "Las ruinas circulares."

417. *Cuentos fantásticos argentinos. Segunda serie.* Selección de Nicolás Cócaro y Antonio E. Serrano Redonnet. [Buenos Aires:] Emecé Editores, [1976].
[1-8] 9-274 [275-284] p. 18.5 cm.

First edition. Includes Borges' "La casa de Asterión."

418. *Diálogos sobre la vida y la muerte. Jorge Luis Borges, J. Severino Croatto, Abel N. Canónico, Alfredo J. Gazzano, Terencio Gioia, Abelardo Castillo.* Coordinadora: Liliana Heker. [Buenos Aires:] Grupo Editor de Buenos Aires S.A., [1980].
[1-6] 7-123 [124-128] p. 20 cm.
(Colección prisma, 20.)

419. *Diez cuentos policiales argentinos. Borges, Hurtado, Marull, Pérez Zelaschi, Peyrou, Eisen, Mayfer, J. del Rey, Bioy, Walsh.* Selección y noticia previa de Rodolfo J. Walsh. Buenos Aires: Librería Hachette, S.A., [1953].
[1-7] 8-190 [191-192] p. 19 cm.
("Evasión," 29.)

Includes Borges' *El jardín de senderos que se bifurcan*, and *Las previsiones de Sangiacomo* by H. Bustos Domecq (pseud.).

420. Flores, Angel

Spanish Stories. Cuentos españoles. New York: Bantam Books, [1960].
[i-vi] vii-xii, [1] 2-339 [340] p. 18 cm.
(A Bantam Dual-Language Book.)

Borges' "La forma de la espada" begins on p. 224. Includes brief biography of the author.

421. *La generación poética de 1922, antología. J. L. Borges, L. Marechal, C. Mastronardi y otros.* Selección, prólogo y notas por la profesora María Raquel Llagostera. [Buenos Aires:] Centro Editor de América Latina, [1980].
[2 unnumbered leaves], i-x, 7-87 [88] p. 18 cm.
(Capítulo, Biblioteca argentina fundamental, 69.)

422. Gerchunoff, Alberto.

Figuras de nuestro tiempo. [Buenos Aires: Editorial Vernácular S.A., 1979].
[1-4] 5-379 [380-384] p. 22.5 cm.
(Serie de grandes inéditos y otras páginas perdurables.)

Includes article by Borges, pp. 11-16: "Borges conversa sobre Gerchunoff."

423. González-Carbalho, José.

Indice de la poesía argentina contemporánea. Santiago: Ediciones Ercilla, 1937.
[iii-ix] x-xiii [xiv-xvii], 18-418 p. 21 cm.
(Colección "Biblioteca América.")

Includes 8 poems by Borges. Special binding. Lacks first leaf [pp. 1-2] and last leaf [pp. 419-420].

BECCO 751

424. Hofstadter, Douglas R.

The Mind's I. Fantasies and Reflections on Self and Soul. Composed and arranged by Douglas R. Hofstadter and Daniel C. Dennett. [Brighton:] The Harvester Press, [1981].
[i-v] vi-vii [viii-x], [1-3] 4-501 [502] p. 24 cm.

Contains two selections by Borges: "Borges and I" and "The Circular Ruins."

425. *La moderna poesía lírica rioplatense (desde Julio Herrera y Reissig y Leopoldo Lugones, hasta nuestros días).* Compilado por Alvaro Yunque y Roberto Zarilli. Buenos Aires: Editorial Futuro, [1944].
[1-4] 5-247 [248] p. 23.5 cm.
(Colección Eurindia, 4.)

Contains Borges' "La fundación mitológica de Buenos Aires" and "Montevideo."

426. *Poesía latinoamericana del siglo XX.* Tomo I. Selección de Susana Zanetti. [Buenos Aires:] Centro Editor de América Latina, [1970].
[1-4] 5-126 [127-128] p. 17 cm.

Includes Borges' "Poema conjetural" and "Poema de los dones."

427. Santiago, José Alberto.

Antología de la poesía argentina. [Madrid: Editora Nacional, 1973].
[1-8] 9-466 [467-468] p. 21 cm.

428. Suárez Calimano, Emilio.

21 ensayos. Jorge Luis Borges. Arturo Lagorio. Francisco López Merino. Eduardo Barrios. Francisco Contreras. Gabriela Mistral. María Monvel. Pedro Prado. A. Hernández Catá. Carlos Loveira. Luis Araquistaín. Alfonso Danvila. Alonso Quesada. Enrique González Martínez. Alfonso Reyes. Alberto Hidalgo. Juana de Ibarbourou. R. Francisco Mazzoni. Vicente A. Salaverri. R. Blanco Fombona. Versos de mujeres. Buenos Aires: Edición de "Nosotros," 1926.
[1-6] 7-198 [199-208] p. 18 cm.

429. *Los universos vislumbrados. Antología de cienciaficción argentina. Bajarlía. Bioy Casares. Boido. Borges. Dabove. Fernández. Gandolfo. Gorodischer. Grassi. Mouján Oteaño. Sábato. Suárez. Vanasco.* Selección y notas de Jorge A. Sánchez. [Buenos Aires:] Ediciones Andrómeda, [1978].
[1-10] 11-294 [295-296] p. 18 cm.
(Colección más allá.)

430. *Variaciones sobre un tema de Durero. Stephen Vincent Benét. Jorge Luis Borges. Haroldo Conti. Marco Denevi. Los Hermanos Grimm. Liliana Heker. Juan José Hernández. Vlady Kociancich. Juan José Mananta. Silvina Ocampo. Oski. Horacio Quiroga.* [Buenos Aires:] Editorial Galerna, [1968].
[1-7] 8-127 [128] p. 20 cm.
(Serie mayor/letras; variaciones, 2.)

Contains "Ritter, Tod und Teufel" by Borges.

431. *Veinte cuentos humorísticos argentinos.* Selección y prólogo de Juan Cicco. Buenos Aires: Librería Huemul, [1972].
[1-7] 8-229 [230-232] p. 18 cm.

Contains "Los ociosos" by Honorio Bustos Domecq (pseud.). Vocabulary follows text.

432. Vignale, Pedro-Juan.

Exposición de la actual poesía argentina. Pedro-Juan Vignale y César Tiempo. Buenos Aires: Ediciones Tres Tiempos, [1977].
[3 unnumbered leaves], [1-4], i-xviii, [5-6] 7-256 [257-264] p. 19.5 cm.
(Colección de poesía "La rosa del sur," 1.)

Facsimile of 1927 edition. Includes six poems by Borges, pp. 93-98.

433. Vignale, Pedro-Juan.

Exposición de la actual poesía argentina (1922-1927). Organizada por Pedro-Juan Vignale y César Tiempo. Buenos Aires: Editorial Minerva, [1927].
[1-4], i-xviii, [5-6] 7-256 [257-268] p. 18.5 cm.

3 copies. One copy is casebound. Includes an autobiography of Borges and several poems previously published in *Fervor de Buenos Aires* and *Luna de enfrente*. Volume also contains poems by Lysandro Z. D. Galtier, who originally owned this copy. First edition, one copy with gray covers. At least one variant state exists with green covers and differing advertisements. Two examples are in this collection. A facsimile reprint of this scarce work was published in 1977 by Ediciones Tres Tiempos of Buenos Aires. Size of second copy, 19 cm.

434. Yahni, Roberto

70 años de narrativa argentina: 1900-1970. Madrid: Alianza Editorial, [1970].
[1-6] 7-212 [213-216] p. 18 cm.
(El libro de bolsillo [267]. Sección: Literatura.)

435. *Zuid Amerikaanse misdaadverbalen*. Verzameld, geredigeerd en van een nawoord voorgien door Erik Lankester. Amsterdam: Loeb, Uitgevers, [1982].
[1-6] 7-251 [252-256] p. 21.5 cm.

Includes “De dood en het kompas” by Borges and “De twaulf tekens van de dierenriem” by Bustos Domecq (pseud.).

VI. COLLABORATIONS

436. Borges, Jorge Luis.

Gli altri. Borges. Bioy Casares. Santiago. Prefazione di Gilles Deleuze, traduzione di Armando Marchi. [Brescia:] Shakespeare & Company, [1981].
[1-6] 7-77 [78-80] p. 20 cm.

First edition. Italian translation of: *Les autres.*

437. Borges, Jorge Luis.

Antiguas literaturas germánicas. Con la colaboración de Delia Ingenieros. México-Buenos Aires: Fondo de Cultura Económica, [1951].
[1-6] 7-179 [180-188] p. 17.5 cm.
(Breviarios del Fondo de Cultura Económica, 53.)

First edition. 2 copies.

BECCO 112

438. Borges, Jorge Luis.

Antiguas literaturas germánicas. Por Jorge Luis Borges con la colaboración de Delia Ingenieros. México-Buenos Aires: Fondo de Cultura Económica, [1965, c. 1951]. [1-6] 7-179 [180-188] p. 17 cm.
(Breviarios del Fondo de Cultura Económica, 53.)

Second edition.

BECCO 113

439. Borges, Jorge Luis.

Antología de la literatura fantástica. Jorge Luis Borges. Silvina Ocampo. Adolfo Bioy Casares. Buenos Aires: Editorial Sudamericana, [1940].
[1-7] 8-328 [329-332] p. 20.5 cm.

(Colección laberinto, 1.)

BECCO 133

440. Borges, Jorge Luis.

Antología de la literatura fantástica. Jorge Luis Borges. Silvina Ocampo. Adolfo Bioy Casares. Buenos Aires: Editorial Sudamericana, [1965]. [1-6] 7-435 [436-440] p. 16.5 cm. (Colección piragua; cuentos, 100.)

BECCO 135

441. Borges, Jorge Luis.

Antologia della letteratura fantastica. Jorge Luis Borges. Silvina Ocampo. Adolfo Bioy Casares. [Rome:] Editori Riuniti, [1981]. [i-iv] v-xxii, [1-2] 3-605 [606] p. 22.5 cm. (Albatros.)

First edition. Italian translation of: *Antología de la literatura fantástica.*

442. Borges, Jorge Luis.

Antología poética argentina. Jorge Luis Borges. Silvina Ocampo. Adolfo Bioy Casares. Buenos Aires: Editorial Sudamericana, [1941]. [1-7] 8-303 [304] p. 20.5 cm. (Colección laberinto, 2.)

3 copies. One copy lacks cover text, including series note.

BECCO 137

443. Borges, Jorge Luis.

Atlante. Con la collaborazione di Maria Kodama. A cura di Domenico Porzio e Hado Lyria.

[Milano:] Arnoldo Mondadori Editore, [1985].
[1-4] 5-74 [75-80] p. 24 cm.

Italian translation of: *Atlas.*

444. Borges, Jorge Luis.

Atlas. Colaboración de María Kodama. [Buenos Aires:] Editorial Sudamericana, [1984].
[1-6] 7-91 [92-96] p. 23 cm.

First edition.

445. Borges, Jorge Luis.

Atlas. In collaboration with Maria Kodama. Translated and annotated by Anthony Kerrigan. New York: E. P. Dutton, [1985].
[1-4] 5-95 [96] p. 23 cm.

English translation of: *Atlas.*

446. Borges, Jorge Luis.

Les autres. Scénario original de Jorge Luis Borges, Adolfo Bioy Casares, et Hugo Santiago. Paris: Christian Bourgois Editeur, [1974].
[1-8] 9-179 [180-192] p. 20 cm.

447. Borges, Jorge Luis.

Het boek van de denkbeeldige wezens. In samenwerking met Margarita Guerrero. Vertaling Annie Sillevis. Amsterdam: De Bezige Bij, 1976.
[1-4] 5-234 [235-240] p. 20.5 cm.
(BB literair.)

Dutch translation of: *El libro de los seres imaginarios.*

448. Borges, Jorge Luis.

The Book of Imaginary Beings. Jorge Luis Borges with Margarita Guerrero. Revised, enlarged, and translated by Norman Thomas di Giovanni in collaboration with the author. New York: E. P. Dutton & Co., Inc., 1969.
[1-6] 7-256 p. 24 cm.

First edition. English translation of: *El libro de los seres imaginarios*. Gift of Joan St. C. Crane.

BECCO 278

449. Borges, Jorge Luis.

The Book of Imaginary Beings. Jorge Luis Borges with Margarita Guerrero. Revised, enlarged and translated by Norman Thomas di Giovanni, in collaboration with the author. London: Jonathan Cape, [1970].
[1-10] 11-256 p. 22.5 cm.

BECCO 279

450. Borges, Jorge Luis.

Borges cantado. Poemas de Jorge Luis Borges con música de Eladia Blázquez, Facundo Cabral, Alberto Cortez, Eduardo Falú, Carlos Guastavino, Jairo, Gustavo Leguizamón, Horacio Malvicino, Rodolfo Mederos, Astor Piazzolla, Daniel Piazzolla, Julián Plaza. Con ilustraciones de Héctor Basaldúa. Transliteración María Clotilde Rezzano de Martini. [Buenos Aires:] Editorial Lago, [1976].
1-104 p. 30 cm.
(Colección canción estampa.)

451. Borges, Jorge Luis.

Borges. Irish Strategies. Two stories by Borges adapted into English by Anthony Kerrigan and into Irish by Diarmaid O Súilleabháin. Two poems in

Spanish on Joyce by Borges with English translations by Anthony Kerrigan. Statements by Borges and Robert Graves. An essay in Irish and in English by Diarmaid O Súilleabháin. A mnemonic note, two essays and a poem on Borges by Anthony Kerrigan. Eight drawings by Bernard Childs. Edited by Liam Miller. [Dublin: Dolmen Press Limited, 1975].
[1-8] 9-87 [88] p. 24.5 cm.
(Dolmen editions, 21.)

In slipcase. First edition, copy number 215 of 350. Autographed.

452. Borges, Jorge Luis.

La cattedrale della paura. Due secoli di racconti polizieschi. Jorge Luis Borges. Adolfo Bioy Casares. [Rome:] Editori Riuniti, [1983].
[1-10] 11-285 [286-288] p. 22.5 cm.
(Albatros.)

First edition. Italian translation of: *Los mejores cuentos policiales. Primera serie.*

453. Borges, Jorge Luis.

Chronicles of Bustos Domecq. Jorge Luis Borges, Adolfo Bioy-Casares. Translated by Norman Thomas di Giovanni. New York: E. P. Dutton & Co., Inc., 1976.
[1-12] 13-143 [144] p. 24 cm.

First edition. 2 copies. English translation of: *Crónicas de Bustos Domecq.* One copy, gift of Joan St. C. Crane. A second copy is signed: "Jorge Luis Borges."

454. Borges, Jorge Luis.

Cielo e inferno. Di Jorge Luis Borges e Adolfo Bioy Casares. Presentazione di Roger Callois. [Parma:] Franco Maria Ricci, 1972.
[1-12] 13-264 [265-272] p. 23.5 cm.

(Morgana, 3.)

Italian translation of: *Libro del cielo y del infierno.* First edition. Number 679 of 2,000 copies.

BECCO 301

455. Borges, Jorge Luis.

El compadrito. Jorge Luis Borges. Silvina Bullrich. Dibujos de Horacio Cardo. Buenos Aires: Compañía General Fabril Editora, S. A., [1968]. [1-6] 7-141 [142-144] p. 28.5 cm.

Second edition. 2 copies.

BECCO 130

456. Borges, Jorge Luis.

El compadrito. Su destino, sus barrios, su música. Buenos Aires: Emecé Editores, S. A., [1945]. [1-6] 7-108 [109-116] p. 18 cm. (Colección buen aire, 64.)

First edition. Compiled by Borges in collaboration with Silvina Bullrich Palenque. Contains 3 plates in text.

BECCO 129

457. Borges, Jorge Luis.

Crónicas de Bustos Domecq. Jorge Luis Borges. Adolfo Bioy Casares. Buenos Aires: Editorial Losada, S. A., [1967]. [1-8] 9-145 [146-148] p. 20 cm. (Colección prisma.)

First edition.

BECCO 97

458. Borges, Jorge Luis.

Crónicas de Bustos Domecq. Jorge Luis Borges. Adolfo Bioy Casares. Buenos Aires: Editorial Losada, S. A., [1968, c. 1967].
[1-10] 11-147 [148-152] p. 20 cm.
(Colección prisma.)

Second edition.

BECCO 98

459. Borges, Jorge Luis.

4 canciones porteñas. Jorge Luis Borges. Astor Piazzolla. Ilustración de Héctor Basaldúa. [Buenos Aires: Editorial Pigal, 1968].
[i-iii], [1] 2-8 [9] p. 32 cm.

Includes: "Alguién le dice al tango," "Jacinto Chiclana," "El títere," and "A don Nicanor Paredes."

BECCO 311

460. Borges, Jorge Luis.

Cuentos breves y extraordinarios (*antología*). Jorge Luis Borges. Adolfo Bioy Casares. Buenos Aires: Santiago Rueda--Editor, [1970, c. 1967].
[1-8] 9-146 [147-148] p. 17.5 cm.
(Colección mundial Rueda, 2.)

[BECCO 125]

461. Borges, Jorge Luis.

Diálogos. Jorge Luis Borges. Ernesto Sábato. [Buenos Aires:] Emecé Editores, [1976].
[3-12] 13-198 [199-202] p. 18.5 cm.

First edition. Lacks first leaf.

462. Borges, Jorge Luis.

Dos fantasías memorables. Jorge Luis Borges. Adolfo Bioy Casares. Edición, notas y bibliografía de Horacio Jorge Becco. Buenos Aires: Edicom, S. A., [1971].
[1-10] 11-79 [80] p. 19.5 cm.
(Letras.)

2 copies.

BECCO 102

463. Borges, Jorge Luis.

"Dos fantasías memorables." (In: *La torre de papel*, no. 1, pp. 9-24. Buenos Aires, June-July 1980).

Appears in "Cuentos" section and contains two short stories: "El testigo" and "El signo." Adolfo Bioy Casares collaborated with Borges on these stories.

464. Borges, Jorge Luis.

Einhorn, Sphinx und Salamander. Buch der imaginären Wesen. In Zusammenarbeit mit Margarita Guerrero. Nach den Übersetzungen von Ulla de Herrera und Edith Aron, bearbeitet und ergänzt von Gisbert Hoefs. Nachwort von Dietmar Kamper. [München:] Carl Hanser Verlag, [1982].
[1-6] 7-171 [172] p. 19 cm.
(Gesammelte Werke, 8.)

German translation of: *El libro de los seres imaginarios.*

[BECCO 241]

465. Borges, Jorge Luis.

Essai sur les anciennes littératures germaniques. Par J. L. Borges et M. E. Vázquez. [Paris: Union Général d'Editions, 1970, c. 1966].

[1-6] 7-190 [191-192] p. 18 cm.
(10"18, 507.)

French translation of: *Antiguas literaturas germánicas.*

[BECCO 250]

466. Borges, Jorge Luis.

Essai sur les littératures médiévales germaniques. Jorge Luis Borges. M. E. Vázquez. Traduit de l'espagnol par Michel Maxence. Paris: Christian Bourgois Editeur, [1981, c. 1966].
[1-6] 7-235 [236-240] p. 20 cm.

French translation of: *Antiguas literaturas germánicas.*

[BECCO 256]

467. Borges, Jorge Luis.

Extraordinary Tales. Jorge Luis Borges, Adolfo Bioy Casares. Edited and translated with a foreword by Anthony Kerrigan. [New York:] Herder and Herder, [1971].
[1-6] 7-144 p. 21 cm.

English translation of: *Cuentos breves y extraordinarios.* Gift of Joan St. C. Crane.

BECCO 286

468. Borges, Jorge Luis.

"The God of the Bulls." (In: *The American Poetry Review*, Vol. 10, no. 1, pp. 23-26. Philadelphia, January-February 1981).

Done in collaboration with Adolfo Bioy Casares.

469. Borges, Jorge Luis.

La hermana de Eloísa. Jorge Luis Borges. Luisa M. Levinson. Buenos Aires: Ene Editorial, [1955]. [1-6] 7-71 [72-80] p. 19.5 cm. (Sección ficción.)

BECCO 114

470. Borges, Jorge Luis.

"El hijo de su amigo." (In: *Eco*, Vol. XXVI, no. 155, pp. 286-307. Bogotá, [1973]).

Done in collaboration with Adolfo Bioy Casares.

471. Borges, Jorge Luis.

El idioma de los argentinos. Jorge Luis Borges. José Edmundo Clemente. Buenos Aires: Peña del Guidice-Editores, [1953, c. 1952]. [1-6] 7-59 [60-64] p. 18 cm. (Colección el ensayo americano, 1.)

2 copies. Includes an essay by Clemente.

BECCO 53

472. Borges, Jorge Luis.

Introdução à literatura inglesa. Jorge Luis Borges em colaboração com María Esther Vázquez. Tradução de Helder Moura Pereira. Posfácio de Gil Nozes de Carvalho. [Lisboa:] Contexto, [1984]. [1-4] 5-77 [78-80] p. 23 cm. (Revisto, 2.)

473. Borges, Jorge Luis.

Introducción a la literatura inglesa. Jorge Luis Borges. En colaboración con María Esther Vázquez. [Buenos Aires:] Editorial Columba, [1965].
[1-6] 7-66 [67-68] p. 20 cm.
(Colección esquemas, 64.)

First edition. 2 copies.

BECCO 115

474. Borges, Jorge Luis.

Introducción a la literatura norteamericana. Jorge Luis Borges (de la Universidad de Buenos Aires). En colaboración con Esther Zamborain de Torres. [Buenos Aires:] Editorial Columba, [1967].
[1-8] 9-67 [68] p. 20 cm.
(Colección esquemas, 77.)

First edition.

BECCO 117

475. Borges, Jorge Luis.

Introduction à la litterature nord-americaine. Traduit de l'espagnol par Luis Jiménez Olivier. [Lausanne:] L'Age d'Homme, [1973].
[1-8] 9-125 [126-128] p. 21 cm.
(Collection la voie ouverte.)

French translation of: *Introducción a la literatura norteamericana*, done in collaboration with Esther Zemborain de Torres.

476. Borges, Jorge Luis.

An Introduction to American Literature. In collaboration with Esther Zemborain de Torres.

New York: Schocken Books, [1973].
[i-vi] vii-x [xi-xii], [1-2] 3-94 [95-100] p. 20 cm.

English translation of: *Introducción a la literatura norteamericana.* Gift of Joan St. C. Crane.

[BECCO 283]

477. Borges, Jorge Luis.

El lenguaje de Buenos Aires. Jorge Luis Borges. José Edmundo Clemente. Buenos Aires: Emecé Editores, [1965, c. 1963].
[1-15] 16-102 [103-104] p. 18.5 cm.
(Selección Emecé de obras contemporáneas.)

Second printing.

[BECCO 54]

478. Borges, Jorge Luis.

Leopoldo Lugones. Buenos Aires: Editorial Trognel, [1955].
[1-8] 9-99 [100-104] p. 20 cm.
(Diálogos del presente, 5.)

Joint author: Betina Edelberg.

BECCO 105

479. Borges, Jorge Luis.

Libro del cielo y del infierno. Jorge Luis Borges. Adolfo Bioy Casares. Buenos Aires: Sur, [1960].
[i-ii], [1-6] 7-215 [216-218] p. 20.5 cm.

First edition. 2 copies.

BECCO 127

480. Borges, Jorge Luis.

Libro del cielo y del infierno. Jorge Luis Borges. Adolfo Bioy Casares. Buenos Aires: Sur, [1970].

[1-11] 12-133 [134-136] p. 17.5 cm. (Colección índice.)

Second edition.

BECCO 128

481. Borges, Jorge Luis.

El libro de los seres imaginarios. Jorge Luis Borges. Con la colaboración de Margarita Guerrero. Ilustraciones de Baldessari. [Buenos Aires:] Editorial Kier, [1967].
[1-6] 7-159 [160] p. 25 cm.

First edition. 2 copies.

BECCO 111

482. Borges, Jorge Luis.

Literaturas germánicas medievales. Jorge Luis Borges. María Esther Vázquez. Buenos Aires: Falbo Librero Editor, [1966, c. 1965].
[1-6] 7-197 [198-208] p. 16.5 cm.
(Colección de las palabras.)

First edition. 2 copies. One copy has autograph: "Jorge Luis Borges."

BECCO 116

483. Borges, Jorge Luis.

Literaturas germánicas medievales. Jorge Luis Borges con la colaboración de María Esther Vázquez. [Buenos Aires:] Emecé Editores, [1978].
[1-6] 7-196 [197-200] p. 18.5 cm.

[BECCO 116]

484. Borges, Jorge Luis.

Manual de zoología fantástica. Por Jorge Luis Borges y Margarita Guerrero. México-Buenos Aires: Fondo de Cultura Económica, [1957].
[1-6] 7-159 [160-168] p. 17.5 cm.
(Breviarios del Fondo de Cultura Económica, 125.)

First edition. 2 copies.

BECCO 108

485. Borges, Jorge Luis.

Manuel de zoologie fantastique. Jorge Luis Borges. Margarita Guerrero. Traduit de l'espagnol par Gonzalo Estrada et Yves Péneau. Dessins originaux de Rodolfo Nieto. Paris: Christian Bourgois Editeur, [1980].
[1-8] 9-195 [196-208] p. 20 cm.

French translation of: *Manual de zoología fantástica.*

[BECCO 255]

486. Borges, Jorge Luis.

Manuale di zoologia fantastica. Jorge Luis Borges e Margarita Guerrero. Traduzione di Franco Lucentini. [Torino:] Einaudi, [1979, c. 1962].
[1-6] 7-163 [164-168] p. 19.5 cm.
(Nuovi coralli, 227.)

Italian translation of: *Manual de zoología fantástica.*

[BECCO 294]

487. Borges, Jorge Luis.

El "Martín Fierro." Con la colaboración de Margarita Guerrero. [Buenos Aires:] Editorial Columba, [1953].

[1-6] 7-79 [80] p. 20.5 cm.
(Colección esquemas, 2.)

First edition. 2 copies.

BECCO 107

488. Borges, Jorge Luis.

El "Martín Fierro." Con la colaboración de Margarita Guerrero. [Buenos Aires:] Emecé Editores, [1979].
[1-6] 7-84 [85-88] p. 17.5 cm.

489. Borges, Jorge Luis.

Los mejores cuentos policiales. Selección y traducción de Adolfo Bioy Casares y Jorge Luis Borges. Buenos Aires: Emecé Editores, S.A., [1947, c. 1943].
[1-8] 9-293 [294-304] p. 19.5 cm.

Third edition.

[BECCO 119]

490. Borges, Jorge Luis.

Los mejores cuentos policiales. Selección de Jorge Luis Borges y Adolfo Bioy Casares. Buenos Aires: Emecé Editores, [1965, c. 1962].
[1-8] 9-299 [300-308] p. 17 cm.
(Colección piragua, 48.)

Fifth edition.

[BECCO 121]

491. Borges, Jorge Luis.

Un modello per la morte. Jorge Luis Borges. Adolfo Bioy Casares. Introduzione di Vanni

Blengino. [Roma:] Editori Riuniti, [1981, c. 1980].
[1-6] 7-88 [89-91] p. 20 cm.
(I David, 52.)

Second edition. Italian translation of: *Un modelo para la muerte.*

492. Borges, Jorge Luis.

Un modelo para la muerte. Jorge Luis Borges. Adolfo Bioy Casares. Buenos Aires: Edicom, S.A., [1970].
[1-7] 8-122 [123-128] p. 19.5 cm.

BECCO 104

493. Borges, Jorge Luis.

Norah. Con quindici litografie di Norah Borges. [Milano:] Edizioni Il Polifilio, [1977].
[i-iv], [1-8] 9-18, [20 unnumbered leaves], 27-44 [45-52] p. 34 cm.

One of 12 special copies of an edition of 500, with an original lithograph laid in. This copy is accompanied by the original for the fifth plate, "El mapamundi." A second copy (printed) of plate VI, "Niños asomándose," is laid in also.

494. Borges, Jorge Luis.

Nouveaux contes de Bustos Domecq. Jorge Luis Borges et Adolfo Bioy Casares. Taduits de l'espagnol par Eduardo Jiménez. Paris: Editions Robert Laffont, [1984].

[1-6] 7-201 [202-208] p. 21.5 cm.
(Pavillons.)

French translation of: *Nuevos cuentos de Bustos Domecq.*

495. Borges, Jorge Luis.

Nuevos cuentos de Bustos Domecq. Jorge Luis Borges. Adolfo Bioy Casares. Ilustraciones de Fernández Chelo. Buenos Aires: Ediciones Librería La Ciudad, [1977].
[1-8] 9-152 [153-160] p. 23 cm.

First edition. Number 3,317 of 4,000 copies.

496. Borges, Jorge Luis.

Obras completas en colaboración. [Buenos Aires:] Emecé Editores, [1979].
[1-14] 15-989 [990-992] p. 22 cm.

First edition. Includes frontispiece portrait of Borges on unnumbered leaf. 2 copies.

497. Borges, Jorge Luis.

Los orilleros. El paraíso de los creyentes. Jorge Luis Borges y Adolfo Bioy Casares. Buenos Aires: Editorial Losada, S.A., [1955].
[1-6] 7-137 [138-140] p. 20.5 cm.
(Novelistas de España y América.)

First edition. 2 copies.

BECCO 96

498. Borges, Jorge Luis.

Los orilleros. El paraíso de los creyentes. Jorge Luis Borges. Adolfo Bioy Casares. Buenos Aires: Editorial Losada, S. A., [1975, c. 1955].
[1-6] 7-137 [138-140] p. 18 cm.
(Biblioteca clásica y contemporánea Losada, 126.)

Second edition.

[BECCO 96]

499. Borges, Jorge Luis.

Poema conjetural. Milonga criolla. Música, Silvia Zimmermann. Letra, Jorge Luis Borges. Buenos Aires: Ediciones Internacionales Fermata, 1969.
2 unnumbered leaves [pp. 1-4]. 31 cm.

Sheet music with lyrics by Borges.

500. Borges, Jorge Luis.

Poesía gauchesca. I-II. Edición, prólogo, notas y glosario de Jorge Luis Borges y Adolfo Bioy Casares. México-Buenos Aires: Fondo de Cultura Económica, [1955].
v. 1: [i-vi] vii-xxvii [xxviii], [1] 2-633 [634-636] p. 22 cm. v. 2: [1-6] 7-798 [799-800] p. 22 cm.
(Biblioteca americana, 29-30. Serie de literatura moderna.)

First edition.

BECCO 126

501. Borges, Jorge Luis.

"Proclama." (In: *Prisma; revista mural,* no. 1. Buenos Aires, December 1921).

This early Ultraist manifesto was also signed by Guillermo de Torre, Guillermo Juan, and Eduardo González Lanuza.

502. Borges, Jorge Luis.

Qué es el budismo. [Buenos Aires:] Editorial Columba, [1976].
[1-5] 6-79 [80] p. 19.5 cm.
(Colección esquemas, 118.)

Joint author: Alicia Jurado. 2 copies.

503. Borges, Jorge Luis.

Qu'est-ce que le buddhisme? Jorge Luis Borges. Alicia Jurado. Traduit de l'espagnol par Françoise-Marie Rosset. [Paris:] Gallimard, [1979].
[1-11] 12-124 [125-128] p. 18 cm.
(Collection idées, 404.)

504. Borges, Jorge Luis.

I signori del misterio. Antologia dei migliori racconti polizieschi. Jorge Luis Borges. Adolfo Bioy Casares. [Rome:] Editori Riuniti, [1982].
[1-10] 11-364 [365-368] p. 22 cm.

Italian translation of: *Los mejores cuentos policiales.*

505. Borges, Jorge Luis.

Six Problems for Don Isidro Parodi. Jorge Luis Borges. Adolfo Bioy Casares. Translated by Norman Thomas di Giovanni. [London:] Allen Lane, [1981].
[1-4] 5-160 p. 24 cm.

English translation of: *Seis problemas para don Isidro Parodi.*

506. Bustos Domecq, H. [pseud.].

"Un après-midi avec Ramón Bonavena." (In: *Cahiers de L'Herne*, no. 4, pp. 71-74. Paris, 1964).

Appears in "Textes inédits" section. 3 copies.

507. Bustos Domecq, H. [pseud.].

Dos fantasías memorables. Buenos Aires: Oportet & Haereses, 1946.
[1-9] 10-34 [35-36] p. 23.5 cm.

Published under pseudonym H. Bustos Domecq (shared with Adolfo Bioy Casares). 2 copies. One copy is number 213 of 300 copies. Contains author's autograph inscription: "Bustos alias/Jorge Luis Borges." Second copy is number 71. Contains inscription: "A Leonidas Barletta,/con un abrazo de/ H. Bustos Domecq." Borges has done only the "H. Bustos" in his own hand, with the remainder of the inscription by Adolfo Bioy Casares. Also contains note written by Lysandro Z. D. Galtier: "Doctor: diviértase/un rato con esta/curiosidad literaria/LG."

BECCO 101

508. Bustos Domecq, H. [pseud.].

"Homenaje a César Paladión." (In: *Sur*, no. 288, pp. [1]-3. Buenos Aires, May-June 1964).

509. Bustos Domecq, H. [pseud.].

"Las noches de Goliadkin." (In: *Sur*, Año XII, no. 90, pp. [34]-50. Buenos Aires, March 1942).

510. Bustos Domecq, H. [pseud.].

Seis problemas para don Isidro Parodi. Palabra liminar de Gersavio Montenegro. Buenos Aires: Sur, [1942].
[1-6] 7-164 [165-172] p. 21 cm.

First edition, bound copy. Bustos Domecq is a pseudonym for Jorge Luis Borges and Adolfo Bioy Casares. Inscribed: "Para Alfredo y/ Marieta, con/ la amistad de/ H. Bustos Domecq."

BECCO 99

511. Bustos Domecq, H. [pseud.].

Seis problemas para don Isidro Parodi. Palabra preliminar de Gersavio Montenegro. Buenos Aires: Sur, [1964, c. 1942].
[1-7] 8-124 [125-128] p. 20 cm.
(Sur, 30.)

Second edition. 2 copies. One copy lacks pp. [1-2].

BECCO 100

512. *Indice de la nueva poesía americana.* Prólogo de Alberto Hidalgo, Vicente Huidobro, y Jorge Luis Borges. Buenos Aires: Sociedad de Publicaciones El Inca, 1926.
[1-4] 5-280 [281-288] p. 18.5 cm.
(Ediciones especiales.)

Library binding.

BECCO 202

513. Marenco, Eleodoro.

El gaucho del Rio de la Plata 1800-1900. Témperas de Eleodoro Marenco. Nota de Jorge Luis Borges. Homenaje al Sesquicentenario de la Declaración de la Independencia Argentina. [Buenos Aires: Edición Productos Roche S.A.Q. e I., 1972?].
8 unnumbered leaves [pp. 1-16]. 33 cm.

Borges wrote a 2-page introduction to this advertising portfolio for Roche drug products featuring 5 (of 6?) watercolor reproductions of Argentine gauchos by Marenco.

514. *Patios.* Natalia Kohen acuarelas; textos de Jorge Luis Borges, Alberto Salas y Oscar Steimberg; comentarios críticos de Raúl Chavárri. [Buenos Aires: Ediciones del Retiro, 1981].
[1-8] 9-51 [52-60] p. 28.5 cm.

Contains: "Un patio" by Borges, pp. 11-14. One of 700 copies.

VII. PROLOGUES AND EDITED WORKS

515. Alcorta, Gloria.

La prison de l'enfant. Préface de J. L. Borges. Lithographies de Héctor Basaldúa. Buenos Aires: [Francisco A. Colombo,] 1935.
[1-8] 9-48 [49-56] p. 29.5 cm.

Number 12 of 50 copies. Includes 8 original lithographs by Basaldúa laid in. Signed by Alcorta, Borges, and Basaldúa. Errata slip laid in. This copy was printed for Oliverio Girondo.

BECCO 157

516. Alifano, Roberto.

Sueño que sueña. [Buenos Aires:] Torres Agüero Editor, [1983].
32 unnumbered leaves [pp. 1-64]. 14 cm.

Prologue by Borges.

517. Alvear, Elvira de.

Reposo. Prólogo de Jorge Luis Borges. Litografías de Héctor Basaldúa. Buenos Aires: M. Gleizer, 1934.
[1-12] 13-100 [101-112] p. 21 cm.
(Colección índice, 7.)

One of 500 copies, unnumbered. 2 copies, one with author's inscription: "A Adelina del Carril, de Guiraldes, con/toda mi admiración por su obra, su/ espíritu y su inteligencia despierta./Elvira de Alvear./ Navidad 1935." This copy lacks front cover.

BECCO 160

518. *Antología de la moderna poesía uruguaya, 1900-1927.* Seleccionada por Ildefonso Pereda Valdés. Palabras finales por Jorge Luis Borges. Buenos Aires: El Ateneo, 1927.

[1-9] 10-224 p. 20 cm.

2 copies, one clothbound.

BECCO 217

519. Ascasubi, Hilario.

Paulino Lucero. Aniceto el Gallo. Santos Vega. Selección. [Buenos Aires:] Editorial Universitaria de Buenos Aires, [1964, c. 1960].
[1-6] 7-188 [189-192] p. 18 cm.
(Serie del siglo y medio, 15.)

Prologue by Borges. Third edition.

[BECCO 162]

520. Bioy Casares, Adolfo.

A invenção de Morel. Prólogo de Jorge Luis Borges. Tradução Miguel Serras Pereira e Maria Teresa Sá. Lisboa: Edições Antígona, 1984.
[1-9] 10-142 [143-148] p. 21 cm.

Portuguese translation of: *La invención de Morel* with prologue by Borges.

521. Bioy Casares, Adolfo.

La invención de Morel. Prólogo de Jorge Luis Borges. Buenos Aires: Editorial Losada, S.A., [1940].
[1-8] 9-169 [170-172] p. 21 cm.
(Novelistas de España y América.)

First edition. Inscribed by author: "Al señor Luis Berisse/en alta estima inte-/lectual/Bioy Casares/ nov 1940."

BECCO 164

522. Bioy Casares, Adolfo.

La invención de Morel, novela. Buenos Aires: Emecé Editores, S.A., [1953].
[1-10] 11-154 [155-156] p. 18.5 cm.

Third edition. Contains a prologue by Borges.

BECCO 166

523. Bloy, Léon.

Cuentos descorteses. Selección y prólogo de Jorge Luis Borges. [Buenos Aires: Ediciones Librería La Ciudad, 1978].
[1-6] 7-110 [111-120] p. 23 cm.
(La biblioteca de Babel, 2.)

First edition. Copy number 549 of 4,000.

524. Bombal, María Luisa.

New Islands and Other Stories. Translated by Richard and Lucia Cunningham. New York: Farrar, Strauss, Giroux, [1982].
[i-xii], [1-3] 4-112 [113-116] p. 21 cm.

Contains a short preface by Borges.

525. Bombal, Susana.

Tres domingos. Prólogo de Jorge Luis Borges. Buenos Aires: [Emecé Editores,] 1957.
[1-6] 7-99 [100-104] p. 19 cm.

Contains author's autograph inscription: "Para [?]/ y en el recuerdo de/los que se fueron, esta/ historia/ muy afectuosamente/Susana Bombal/ 1958."

BECCO 168

526. Borges, Jorge Luis.

Buch der Träume. Übersetzt von Curt Meyer-Clason. Nachwort Caroline Neubaur. [München:] Carl Hanser Verlag, [1981].
[1-6] 7-207 [208] p. 19 cm.
(Gesammelte Werke, 7.)

German translation of: *Libro de sueños*.

527. Borges, Jorge Luis.

Libro de sueños. Buenos Aires: Torres Agüero Editor, [1976].
[1-7] 8-152 [153-160] p. 20 cm.
(La flecha de Zenón.)

Writings by other authors. 2 copies.

528. Campo, Estanislao del.

Fausto. Impresiones del gaucho Anastasio el Pollo en la representación de esta obra. Prólogo de Jorge Luis Borges. Edición, notas y vocabulario de Horacio Jorge Becco. Dibujos de Jorge Enrique Werffeli. Buenos Aires: Edicom, S.A., [1969].
[1-8] 9-98 [99-104] p. 27 cm.
(Los arquetipos de la literatura argentina.)

Number 563 of 3,000 copies. Printed by Francisco A. Colombo.

BECCO 176

529. Carriego, Evaristo.

La costurerita que dió aquel mal paso y otros poemas. Buenos Aires: Torres Agüero Editor, [1977].
[1-8] 9-124 [125-144] p. 14 cm.
(Papeles del Andarín.)

Includes an 11-page discussion of Carriego by Borges. 2 copies.

530. Carriego, Evaristo.

Poesías. Misas herejes. La canción del barrio. Prólogo de Jorge Luis Borges. Nota preliminar de José Edmundo Clemente. Ilustraciones de Sigfredo. Buenos Aires: Editorial Renacimiento, 1950. [i-iv], [1-6] 7-197 [198-206] p. 23 cm.

BECCO 180

531. *Cuentos originales. José H. Cibils, Julio C. de la Torre, Carlos Ghiara, S. Oscar Grassi, Jorge Milia, Julio O. Peña, Ubaldo Pérez, Rogelio Pfirter.* Prólogo de Jorge Luis Borges. Santa Fe, Argentina: Librería y Editorial Castellvi, S.A., [1965]. [3-6] 7-78 [79-80] p. 20.5 cm.

At head of title: Departamento de Letras del Colegio de la Inmaculada Concepción.

532. Dabove, Santiago.

La muerte y su traje. Prólogo de Jorge Luis Borges. Buenos Aires: Editorial Alcándara, [1961]. [1-7] 8-138 [139-144] p. 20 cm.

BECCO 188

533. Dante Alighieri.

La divina comedia. Estudio preliminar por Jorge Luis Borges. Traducción de Cayetano Rosell, y notas de Narciso Bruzzi Costas. Buenos Aires: W. M. Jackson, Inc. Editores, [1952]. [i-vi] vii-xxviii, [1-2] 3-503 [504] p. 21 cm. (Clásicos Jackson, 31.)

Second edition. Frontispiece portrait of Dante.

BECCO 158

534. *Emilio Pettoruti. Homenaje nacional a 50 años de labor artística.* [Buenos Aires:] Dirección General de Cultura. Ministerio de Educación y Justicia. Museo Nacional de Bellas Artes, 1962.
[1-5] 6-91 [92] p. 24 cm.

Prologue by Borges.

535. Fernández Latour, Enrique.

Macedonio Fernández candidato a presidente, y otros escritos de Enrique Fernández Latour. Con una carta-prólogo de Jorge Luis Borges. [Buenos Aires:] Ediciones Agon, [1980].
[1-4] 5-64 p. 20 cm.

536. Fernández Moreno, [Baldomero].

Versos de negrita. Buenos Aires: Editorial Deucalión, [1956].
[1-4] 5-144 p. 20 cm.

Prologue by Borges, pp. 5-8.

BECCO 190

537. *El gaucho.* Fotografías de René Burri. Texto de José Luis Lanuza. Prefacio de Jorge Luis Borges. Viñetas de Juan Carlos Castagnino. Diagramación de Paolo Mazzetti. Buenos Aires: Muchnik Editores, [1968].
[1-8] 9-55 [56-176] p. 29.5 cm.

2 copies.

BECCO 174

538. Grondona, Mariana.

Más allá de mi río. Prólogo de Jorge Luis Borges. [Buenos Aires:] Emecé Editores, [1971].
[1-9] 10-264 [265-268] p. 20 cm.

First edition, second printing. 2 copies.

BECCO 196

539. Groussac, Paul.

Lo mejor de Paul Groussac. Jorge Luis Borges, selecciona. Buenos Aires: Editorial Fraterna, [1981].
[i-vi] vii-xi [xii], [1-2] 3-269 [270-276] p. 23 cm.
(Borges selecciona lo mejor de Groussac, 1.)

Prologue by Borges.

540. Grünberg, Carlos M.

Mester de judería. Prólogo de Jorge Luis Borges. Buenos Aires: Editorial Argiropolis, 1940.
[i-viii] ix-xvi [xvii-xviii], 1-153 [154-158] p. 21 cm.

2 copies. One copy contains inscription: "Al Dr. Agustín N. Matiengo,/homenaje del autor./ Grünberg."

BECCO 197

541. Hernández, José.

El gaucho Martín Fierro. La vuelta de Martín Fierro. [Buenos Aires: Ediciones Centurión, 1962].
v. 1: [i-ii], [1-3] 4-78 [79-82] p. 28 cm. v. 2: [1-3] 4-59 [60-64] p. 28.5 cm.

Facsimile reprints of original editions dated 1872 and 1879. Four-page prologue by Borges laid in v. 1. 2 copies. One copy is missing last leaf in both volumes. These contain reprint publisher information, and they were obviously removed in order to create the illusion that the volumes were originals. This copy also was apparently lacking the prologue by Borges, which was later supplied in photocopy. Borges, as Director of the Biblioteca Nacional, supplied the publisher with the originals from which the facsimiles were produced.

BECCO 199

542. Hernández, José.

El gaucho Martín Fierro. La vuelta de Martín Fierro. Barcelona: Carraggio, S.A. de Ediciones, [1980, c. 1953].
[1-7] 8-347 [348-352] p. 23.5 cm.
(Colección clásicos Carraggio.)

"Presentación" by Borges in collaboration with Margarita Guerrero, pp. [5]-[41]. Includes unnumbered leaf with portrait of Hernández following p. [4], and 15 illustrations by Ciro Oduber, also on unnumbered leaves in the text.

543. Hernández, José.

Martín Fierro. Prólogo de Jorge Luis Borges. Buenos Aires: Sur, [1962].
[1-7] 8-130 [131-136] p. 20 cm.

BECCO 200

544. Hernández, José.

Martín Fierro. Buenos Aires: Santiago Rueda-Editor, [1968].
[1-6] 7-246 [247-248] p. 17.5 cm.
(Colección mundial Rueda, 7.)

Introduction by Borges.

BECCO 201

545. Jauretche, Arturo M.

El paso de los libres. [Buenos Aires:] A. Peña Lillo Editor SRL, [1974].
[1-20] 21-88 [89-96] p. 20 cm.

Third edition. Prologue by Borges.

[BECCO 206]

546. Jauretche, Arturo M.

El paso de los libres. Relato gaucho de la última revolución radical (diciembre de 1933) dicho en verso por el paisano Julián Barrientos, que anduvo en ella. Prólogo de Jorge Luis Borges. Buenos Aires: Editorial "La Boina Blanca," [1934].
[1-6] 7-93 [94-98] p. 19.5 cm.

Contains author's autograph inscription: "Para el amigo Tanes,/cordialmente./Bs.As. 21-1-935./AM Jauretche." Bound in cloth for J. F. Tanes (initials at foot of spine).

BECCO 205

547. Kafka, Franz.

El buitre. Selección y prólogo de Jorge Luis Borges. [Buenos Aires: Ediciones Librería La Ciudad, 1979].
[1-6] 7-99 [100-104] p. 22.5 cm.
(La biblioteca de Babel, 6.)

First edition. Copy number 2,956 of 4,000. Translations by Jorge Luis Borges and Miguel Ballesteros Acevedo.

548. Kafka, Franz.

La metamórfosis. Traducción de: Nélida Mendilaharzu de Machain. Buenos Aires: Ediciones Orión, [1982].
[1-4] 5-130 [131-136] p. 17.5 cm.

(Colección alfa de Orión. Narrativa contemporánea.)

Introduction by Borges: "Jorge Luis Borges habla del mundo de Kafka," pp. 5-28.

549. Lange, Norah.

La calle de la tarde. Buenos Aires: J. Samet, Librero-Editor, [1925].
[1-4] 5-62 [63-64] p. 18.5 cm.

Date of 1925 not given in book. Prologue by Borges. One copy contains author's autograph inscription: "Para Emilio Soto/ Cordialmente/ Nora Lange." 2 copies.

BECCO 209

550. *El libro de los autores.* [Buenos Aires:] Ediciones de la Flor, [1967].
[1-7] 8-174 [175-176] p. 20 cm.

Favorite selections of authors, made by Borges (who chooses Nathaniel Hawthorne's *Wakefield*), Mújica Laínez, Sábato, and others.

551. London, Jack.

Las muertes concéntricas. Selección y prólogo de Jorge Luis Borges. [Buenos Aires: Ediciones Librería La Ciudad, 1979].
[1-6] 7-121 [122-132] p. 22.5 cm.
(La biblioteca de Babel, 3.)

Translations by Nora Dottori and Jorge Luis Borges. First edition. Copy number 3,235 of 4,000.

552. Lugones, Leopoldo.

Antología poética. Selección e introducción de Jorge Luis Borges. Madrid: Alianza Editorial, [1982].
[1-6] 7-152 [153-160] p. 18 cm.
(El libro de bolsillo, 885; Sección: literatura.)

553. Lugones, Leopoldo.

Romances del Río Seco. Prólogo de: Jorge Luis Borges. Ilustraciones de: Carlos Alonso. [Córdoba: Alción Editora, 1984].
[1-8] 9-254 [255-256] p. 27 cm.

Contains prologue by Borges. Copy number 667 of 2,000. Boxed.

554. Melville, Herman.

Bartleby el escribiente. Prólogo de Jorge Luis Borges. [Buenos Aires: Ediciones Librería La Ciudad, 1979].
[1-6] 7-67 [68-72] p. 23 cm.
(La biblioteca de Babel, 5.)

Translation by Borges. First edition. Copy number 244 of 4,000.

555. Meyrink, Gustav.

El cardenal Napellus. Selección y prólogo de Jorge Luis Borges. [Buenos Aires: Ediciones Librería La Ciudad, 1979].
[1-6] 7-71 [72-84] p. 23 cm.

First edition. Copy number 3,200 of 4,000.

556. Mújica Laínez, Manuel.

The Wandering Unicorn. Translated by Mary Fitton, with a foreword by Jorge Luis Borges. New York: Taplinger Publishing Company, [1983].
[i-vi] vii [viii-x], 1-322 [323-326] p. 21.5 cm.

First American edition. Original title: *El unicornio.*

557. *El niño y el joven; motores del desarrollo.* R. Esquerra Barry, E. J. R. Heyward, V. R. Montesinos V., C. Satilios-Rothschild. Presentacion por Jorge Luis Borges. Buenos Aires: Paidós-UNICEF, [1972].
[1-7] 8-192 [193-200] p. 18.5 cm.
(Biblioteca del educador contemporáneo. Serie menor, 157.)

558. Nobody, Ulises [pseud.].

El frac. [Buenos Aires:] Emecé Editores, [1961].
[1-11] 12-177 [178-180] p. 20.5 cm.

Prologue by Borges. One copy inscribed: "Al excelente colaborador/Sr. Roberto Gallichio/--con mi franca/simpatía--/[?]/(alias) Ulises Nobody." 2 copies, 1 with dust jacket.

559. Papini, Giovanni.

El espejo que huye. Selección y prólogo de Jorge Luis Borges. [Buenos Aires: Ediciones Librería La Ciudad, 1978].
[1-6] 7-115 [116-120] p. 23 cm.
(La biblioteca de Babel, 1.)

First edition. Copy number 1,340 of 4,000.

BECCO 215

560. *Qué es la Argentina. Guillermo Ana. Romualdo Brughetti. Mariano Castex. Gustavo F. J. Cirigliano. Augusto R. Cortazar. Alfredo J. Grassi. Ismael Quiles. Francisco Valsecchi. Juan Adolfo Vázquez.* Con prólogo de Jorge Luis Borges. [Buenos Aires:] Editorial Columba, [1970].
[1-4] 5-365 [366-368] p. 19.5 cm.
(Colección esquemas, 100.)

BECCO 161

561. Quevedo, Francisco de.

Antología poética. Prólogo y selección de Jorge Luis Borges. Madrid: Alianza Editorial, [1982].
[1-6] 7-143 [144] p. 18 cm.
(El libro de bolsillo, 873; Sección: clásicos.)

562. Quevedo, Francisco de.

Prosa y verso. Buenos Aires: Emecé Editores, S.A., [1948].
[1-6] 7-904 [905-912] p. 18 cm.
(Clásicos Emecé, 17.)

Selections from Quevedo by Borges and Bioy Casares. Borges also wrote the prologue.

BECCO 123

563. Rey, Jean-Dominique.

Guillermo Roux. New York: Rizzoli, [1984]. [1-8] 9-147 [148] p. 33.5 cm.

Contains prologue, “San José de Flores,” by Borges.

564. Risso Platero, Ema.

Arquitecturas del insomnio; cuentos fantásticos. Prólogo de Jorge Luis Borges. Buenos Aires: Ediciones Botella al Mar, [1948].
[1-8] 9-205 [206-208] p. 17.5 cm.
(La sirena escondida.)

Becco cites author as Ema Risso Patrón. 2 copies.

BECCO 220

565. Rosales, Horacio Eduardo.

Recuerdos de la tierra. Buenos Aires: ["NEXO." Galería de Arte y Cultura,] 1966.
[1-8] 9-110 [111- 120] p. 23.5 cm.

Prologue by Borges. Illustrations by Norah Borges and others.

BECCO 221

566. Rossi, Attilio.

Buenos Aires en tinta china. Prólogo de Jorge Luis Borges. Poema de Rafael Alberti. Buenos Aires: Editorial Losada, S.A., [1951].
[1-6] 7-186 [187-192] p. 19.5 cm.
(Biblioteca contemporánea.)

Illustrations by Rossi. 2 copies. One copy lacks pp. [1-4] and dust jacket.

BECCO 222

567. Sarmiento, Domingo F.

Facundo. Edición anotada y comentada por Jorge Luis Borges. Buenos Aires: Librería 'El Ateneo' Editorial, [1974].
[i-vii] viii-xviii, [1] 2-274 [275-276] p. 18.5 cm.
(Libros fundamentales comentados.)

568. Sarmiento, Domingo F.

Recuerdos de provincia. Prólogo y notas de Jorge Luis Borges. Buenos Aires: Emecé Editores, S.A., [1944].
[1-8] 9-320 [321-328] p. 20.5 cm.
(Colección el navío, 1.)

BECCO 224

569. Shakespeare, William.

Macbeth. Translated by Guillermo Whitelaw. Prólogo de Jorge Luis Borges. [Buenos Aires:] Editorial Sudaméricana, [1970].
[1-6] 7-207 [208-212] p. 17.5 cm.
(Colección obras maestras Fondo Nacional de las Artes.)

2 copies.

BECCO 226

570. Thorlichen, Gustav.

La República Argentina. Prólogo de Jorge Luis Borges. Buenos Aires: Nuestro Pabellón, 1958.
[1-4] 5-103 [104] p. 22 cm.

Photographs by the author.

BECCO 227

571. Valéry, Paul.

El cementerio marino. Traducción de Néstor Ibarra. Prefacio de Jorge Luis Borges. Buenos Aires: Ediciones Schellinger, [1931].
[1-4] 5-31 [32-36] p. 24.5 cm.

Copy number 74 of 500 copies. Borges' personal copy, bound in blue cloth with his initials on spine. Contains Borges' autograph corrections in text.

[BECCO 228]

572. Zenner, Wally.

Antigua lumbre. Con un prefacio de Jorge Luis Borges y un dibujo de León Benarós. Buenos Aires: [Francisco A. Colombo,] 1949.
[1-6] 7-60 [61-64] p. 24.5 cm.

Contains author's autograph inscription: "A Inés Malinow./A la pura voz de/su poesia./ Amistosamente/Wally/10/50."

BECCO 235

VIII. TRANSLATIONS BY BORGES

573. *Breve antología anglosajona.* Jorge Luis Borges, María Kodama. [Santiago:] Ediciones La Ciudad, [1978].
[1-6] 7-46 [47-48] p. 23 cm.
(Colección de poesía.)

Spanish translations of early Old English poetry, with commentaries.

574. Faulkner, William.

Las palmeras salvajes. Traducción de Jorge Luis Borges. Buenos Aires: Editorial Sudamericana, [1940].
[1-6] 7-365 [366-368] p. 18.5 cm.
(Colección horizonte.)

Borges' translation of William Faulkner's *The Wild Palms.* One copy bound, 17.5 cm. This copy lacks first leaf. 2 copies.

575. Gide, André.

Perséphone. [Buenos Aires: Sur, 1936].
[i-ii], [1-3] 4-47 [48] p. 24 cm.

Translation from the French by Borges. First printing (in offprint format) by the journal *Sur*, in honor of Igor Stravinsky.

576. "Lepanto." (In: *Sol y luna*, no. 1, pp. 136-147. Buenos Aires, 1938).

Translation by Borges of the original poem by G. K. Chesterton. Alderman Library's Borges Collection contains a complete set of *Sol y luna* (nos. 1-10 and Almanaque, 1938-1940).

577. Michaux, Henri.

Un bárbaro en Asia. [Translated by Jorge Luis Borges]. Barcelona: [Tusquets Editor, 1977].
[1-14] 15-228 [229-232] p. 18.5 cm.
(Marginales, 53.)

578. Whitman, Walt.

Hojas de hierba. Buenos Aires: Juárez Editor, [1969].
[1-8] 9-171 [172-184] p. 31.5 cm.

First edition. One of 2,000 copies on Japanese paper. Borges' translation of Whitman's *Leaves of Grass*, with a prologue also by Borges. 2 copies.

BECCO 231

579. Whitman, Walt.

Hojas de hierba. Selección, traducción y prólogo de Jorge Luis Borges. Estudio crítico de Guillermo Nolasco Juárez. Grabados de Antonio Berni. [Barcelona: Editorial Lumen, 1972].
[1-4] 5-162 [163-168] p. 18.5 cm.
(Palabra menor, 11.)

Borges' translation of Whitman's *Leaves of Grass*. 2 copies.

[BECCO 231]

IX. MANUSCRIPTS

580. Belitt, Ben.

[Papers.] 1967-1978. Handwritten and typed manuscripts, 96 items (various pagings).

This collection contains primarily correspondence between Belitt and Norman Thomas di Giovanni concerning Belitt's translations into English of poems by Borges for the first edition of *Selected Poems, 1923-1967* (1972). Other items include a program for a reading by Giovanni, an introduction for him by Belitt, and an article by Giovanni on working as a translator with Borges. Belitt's working notes for the translations are also part of this material.

581. Borges, Jorge Luis.

"Boletín de una noche." Circa 1924-1926. Autograph manuscript, 2 pages.

This item, with numerous corrections by Borges, was intended as an essay for *El idioma de los argentinos* (1928) but was never published. One of the earliest attempts by Borges to define and analyze his writing as it related to his being and personality.

582. Borges, Jorge Luis.

"La cábala." Circa 1943. Autograph manuscript, signed, 1 page.

Original version of an extremely important text in the Borges canon. Contains many source notes in margins.

583. Borges, Jorge Luis.

"Carta Deshilvanada." Circa 1920s. Autograph manuscript, signed, 2 pages on 1 leaf.

On letterhead of the Hôtel Bayard, rue Richer, Paris.

584. Borges, Jorge Luis.

"La casa de Asterión." 1946. Autograph manuscript, signed, 7 pages.

Includes an autograph letter to Borges from the writer Julio Cortázar praising this short story, which was published in *El aleph* (1949). Contains numerous textual corrections and variants from printed versions.

585. Borges, Jorge Luis.

[Essay on Flaubert.] Circa 1924-1955. Autograph manuscript, 18 pages on 16 leaves.

Portions of this text appeared in "Flaubert y su destino ejemplar" and "Vindicación de Bouvard et Pecuchet." The last 3 pages were dictated to Borges' mother, Leonor Acevedo, and are in her hand. These pages contain the preliminary version of a *milonga* for one Jacinto Chiclana, entitled "Elegía" and written at a much later date than the Flaubert study. The definitive version of this *milonga* was printed in *Para las seis cuerdas* (1965).

586. Borges, Jorge Luis.

"La fundación mitológica de Buenos Aires." Before 1929. Autograph manuscript, signed, 2 pages.

Subtitled: "(imaginada con ninguna imaginación por J. L. Borges)." The text of this manuscript differs significantly from the first published version in *Cuaderno San Martín* (1929).

587. Borges, Jorge Luis.

"Intentona de Soneto." Circa 1920s. Autograph manuscript, signed, 1 page.

Original manuscript, signed with Borges' initials. With 1 marginal note. On the reverse side of the sheet is a letter in Borges' hand, signed: "Georgie."

588. Borges, Jorge Luis.

[Letter.] Circa 1920s. Autograph manuscript, signed, 1 page.

Letter referring to many Argentine writers of the period. Borges also mentions an amusing incident concerning 3 marijuana smokers, the metaphysics of which he compares to a story such as Chesterton might have written.

589. Borges, Jorge Luis.

[Letter.] Circa 1920s. Autograph manuscript, signed, 3 pages.

Signed with Borges' initials. Written at the Argentine Consulate in Madrid, on stationery from the Hotel España in Barcelona.

590. Borges, Jorge Luis.

[Letter.] Circa 1929. Autograph manuscript, signed, 1 page.

Letter to Carlos Mastronardi, signed with Borges' initials. Mentions forthcoming publication of *Cuaderno San Martín* (1929).

591. Borges, Jorge Luis.

[Letter.] October 1962. Manuscript, signed, 1 page, with envelope.

Letter (postmarked Boston) in English, in Borges' mother's hand and signed by Borges, to Ernest T. Manfred of New York, thanking him for his comments on *Labyrinths*.

592. Borges, Jorge Luis.

[Letter.] 19 July 1963. Manuscript, signed, 1 page, with envelope.

Letter in Borges' mother's hand and signed by Borges, to a Mr. Cohen in Tangier. Borges thanks Cohen for his note and comments on his failing eyesight.

593. Borges, Jorge Luis.

"The Mirror and the Mask." 1962. Typescript, signed, 1 page.

Fragment (4 paragraphs) of the original English text.

594. Borges, Jorge Luis.

"El muerto." Before 1949. Autograph manuscript, 13 pages.

Original manuscript, probably supplied to the printer, of a Borges masterpiece. Contains extensive textual corrections and deletions. Later published in *El aleph* (1949).

595. Borges, Jorge Luis.

"La pampa y el suburbio son dioses." Circa 1925. Autograph manuscript, signed, 8 pages.

Original version of a central essay in *El tamaño de mi esperanza* (1926). Includes an autograph letter, dated 25 December 1948, from Ricardo Molinari, a fellow poet from Borges' Ultraist days, conveying the manuscript to an unknown recipient, "mi estimado doctor."

596. Borges, Jorge Luis.

"S.S." January 1959. Typescript, signed, 1 page.

This poem was later retitled and published as "Susana Soca." Includes a letter in Borges' mother's hand and signed by Borges, to the mother of Susana Soca, expressing sympathy on her daughter's death. Both items are on letterhead from Borges' office as director of the Biblioteca Nacional in Buenos Aires.

597. Borges, Jorge Luis.

"Villa Mazzini." Circa 1923. Autograph manuscript, 1 page.

Borges originally intended to publish this poem in his first book, *Fervor de Buenos Aires* (1923). It was withdrawn before publication and has never appeared in print. Villa Mazzini, on Tronador Street in Buenos Aires, was the home of Norah Lange, a poet and close friend of Borges from the early days.

598. Gellius, Aulus.

Noches áticas. Vol. 1. Aulo Gelio. Traducción directa del latín por don Francisco Navarro y Calvo, Canónigo de la Metropolitana de Granada. Madrid: Librería de la viuda de Hernández y Ca., Calle del Arenal, Num. 11, 1893.
[i-iv], 1-393 [394-396] p. 18 cm.
(Biblioteca clásica, CLXIX).

Borges' personal copy of this title, containing the following autograph notes:

a. On verso of half title and front free endpaper, manuscript draft of Borges' essay "Sentirse en muerte," later included in the text of "Nueva refutación del tiempo." This piece is the earliest known record of the author's mystical experience, circa 1926.

b. Facing p. 156, small leaf laid in containing 4 ink drawings by Borges of typical Argentine *compadritos*.

c. On verso of leaf above, pencil sketch of a woman's head, with caption: "Poemas en prosa."

d. On p. [394], outline for contents of *El idioma de los argentinos*, with title notes and some thematic discussion.

e. On recto of final blank, 2 drafts of a book dedication.

f. On recto of final blank, 2 signatures by Borges.

X. MISCELLANY

599. *Los anales de Buenos Aires*. Año I, no. 1-Año III, no. 23. [Buenos Aires, January 1946-January 1948].

Complete set of this journal to which Borges contributed heavily. Borges also served as editor for the magazine. Alderman Library owns 2 copies of the set, one bound in 3 volumes.

600. Bioy Casares, Adolfo.

"On Fantastic Literature." (In: *Tri Quarterly*, no. 25, pp. 222-230. Evanston, Ill., Fall 1972).

Originally published as the introduction to the *Antología de la literatura fantástica*, edited by Borges, Bioy Casares, and Silvina Ocampo in 1940.

601. [Borges], Guillermo Juan.

"Parque." (In: *Proa*, Año I, no. 2, p. [4]. Buenos Aires, December 1922).

602. [Borges], Guillermo Juan.

"Poemas." (In: *Proa*, Año I, no. 1, p. [4]. Buenos Aires, August 1922).

603. Borges, Jorge.

El caudillo. Novela. [Palma de Mallorca: Imprenta Mallorquina de Juan Guasp Reinés,] 1921. [1-3] 4-195 [196] p. 20.5 cm.

Exceedingly rare example of Borges' father's only published work, a novel. Alderman Library owns two copies, one of which has a spine decorated with small designs and rules, with "J. Borges" and "El caudillo" lettered in, all in ink and done by hand.

The other copy, from another source, has no such additions, but preserves its original transparent dust jacket.

604. Borges, Jorge.

"Rubayiat." (In: *Proa*, Año I, no. 5, pp. 55-57. Buenos Aires, December 1924).

Translation by Borges' father.

605. Borges, Jorge.

"Rubayiat (continuación)." (In: *Proa*, Año II, no. 6, pp. 61-68. Buenos Aires, January 1925).

Translation by Borges' father.

606. Borges, Jorge Luis.

"A Borges Family Chronicle." (In: *Tri Quarterly*, no. 25, [4 unnumbered leaves following p. 322]. Evanston, Ill., Fall 1972).

Photographs of Borges and his family, with captions written by the author.

607. Borges, Jorge Luis.

[Folger Library's Shakespeare Birthday Lecture, 23 April 1976.]
1 audiocassette.

Privately prepared tape recording of a speech by Borges at the Folger Shakespeare Library in Washington, D.C. Borges delivered the plenary lecture as part of an international commemorative program for Shakespeare's 412th birthday. The event, titled *Shakespeare in America*, was co-hosted by the Folger Library and the Shakespeare Association of America. Gift of C. Jared Loewenstein.

608. *Borges para millones.* [Videorecording.] Princeton: Films for the Humanities, [1985?].
1 videocassette (70 min.), 1/2 in., VHS format.

Director: Ricardo Wullicher. Producers: Juan Carlos Victoria, Milton Fontaina. Contains an interview with Borges concerning his life and writings. Includes staged reenactments of some of his works.

609. Comesaña, Eduardo.

Fotos poco conocidas de gente muy conocida. Integran esta carpeta las siguientes fotografías: Pedro Eugenio Aramburu, Adolfo Bioy Casares, Jorge Luis Borges, Charles de Gaulle, Roberto de Vicenzo, Eugene Ionesco, Arturo Jauretche, Robert Kennedy, Juan Carlos Onganía, Emilio Pettoruti, Astor Piazzolla, José María Rosa. [Buenos Aires: Imprenta Anzilotti, 1972].
14 unnumbered leaves [pp. 1-28]. 35 cm.

Contains photograph of Borges.

BECCO 1376

610. *Destiempo.* Año I, no. 1-Año I, no. 3. Buenos Aires, October 1936-December 1936.

All published of this literary magazine. Borges contributed to the first and third issues. This title is exceptionally rare, the third (final) issue particularly so.

611. "'Destiempo' se llama una nueva revista de vanguardia literaria . . . " (In: *Nosotros*, Segunda Epoca, Año I, no. 2, p. 247. Buenos Aires, September 1936).

612. *Dichter mit Umgebung*. Fotos: Leonore Mau. Text: Hubert Fichte. [Frankfurt:] Qumran, [1981]. [4 unnumbered leaves, 50 loose photographs, boxed.] 16 x 22 cm. (Portrait, 2.)

A portfolio of literary portrait photographs, including 8 of Borges.

613. Dillard, R. H. W.

"The Past Tense. Three Poems." (In: *Tri Quarterly*, no. 25, pp. 144-148. Evanston, Ill., Fall 1972).

Original poems based on Borges' texts.

614. Gómez de la Serna, Ramón.

Norah Borges. Buenos Aires: Editorial Losada, S.A., [1945]. [i-iv], [1-4] 5-41 [42], [35 unnumbered leaves], [43-46] p. 19 cm. (Monografías de arte. Serie argentina, 7.)

One copy has 8 unnumbered leaves mistakenly duplicated, not included in pagination formula as shown. 2 copies.

615. González Castro, Augusto.

María Josefina de los Angeles. Poema. Buenos Aires: Francisco A. Colombo, 1935. [i-iv], [1-8] 9-99 [100-104] p. 24 cm.

Copy number 1 of 40 copies on special paper. This copy printed especially for Borges. Inscription by author reads: "Jorge Luis Borges,/con la profunda/ estimación de su/compañero/Augusto González Castro/15/1/37."

616. Hollander, John.

"Index: Homage to Borges." (In: *Tri Quarterly*, no. 25, pp. 460-462. Evanston, Ill., Fall 1972).

Poem by Hollander, in the form of a mythical index to one (or more) of Borges' texts.

617. *El hombre de la esquina rosada.* [Videorecording.] Princeton: Films for the Humanities, 1980.
1 videocassette (71 min.), 1/2 in., VHS format.

Director: Germán Quejido. Based on the text by Borges.

618. "Iconographie." (In: *Cahiers de L'Herne*, no. 4, pp. [523-538]. Paris, 1964).

Photographs of Borges and his work. 3 copies.

619. *The Inner World of Jorge Luis Borges.* [Videorecording.] Princeton: Films for the Humanities, [197-?].
1 videocassette (30 min.), 1/2 in., VHS format.

Director/Producer: Harold Mantell. In this film, Borges comments upon the books and places which influenced his writing.

620. "Jorge Luis Borges à Alfonso Reyes." (In: *Cahiers de L'Herne*, no. 4, pp. 55-57. Paris 1964).

Appears in "Correspondance" section. 3 copies.

621. Lange, Norah.

Antes que mueran. Buenos Aires: Editorial Losada, [1944].
[1-6] 7-205 [206-208] p. 21 cm.

(Prosistas de España y América.)

Inscribed by Lange: "Para Clara y Alberto Zum / Felde--estas cosas solitarias, /con la gran estimación y la /amistad de Norah Lange /Nov-15-1944."

622. Loza Aguerrebere, Rubén.

El hombre que robó a Borges. Cuentos. [Montevideo:] Ediciones Menphis, [1979]. [1-6] 7-140 [141-144] p. 17 cm.

623. *Martín Fierro (1924-1927).* Antología y prólogo Beatriz Sarlo Sabajanes. [Buenos Aires:] Carlos Pérez Editor, [1969]. [1-6] 7-189 [190-192] p. 19.5 cm.

Selections from the journal *Martín Fierro,* including 5 of Borges' contributions and a review of *Luna de enfrente* by Leopoldo Marechal. Alderman Library also owns a complete set of the original *Martín Fierro* on microfilm, in the library's general collections.

624. *Poesía;* [*revista internacional de poesía.* Nos. 1/2-6/ 7. Buenos Aires, June-November 1933].

Complete collection of this scarce journal. Alderman Library's set is bound in one volume, with initials of Lysandro Z.D. Galtier at base of spine.

625. *Prisma; revista mural.* [No. 1. Buenos Aires, December 1921].

One of the scarcest of all Borges items, this is the first of two issues of the "mural magazine" which Borges published soon after his return to Argentina from Europe. The little Ultraist poetry broadside was published in a second issue in March 1922. The first number contained 9 poems and a manifesto on the principles of Ultraism, signed by Borges, Guillermo de Torre, Guillermo Juan, and Eduardo González Lanuza. The broadside in Alderman Library's collection measures approximately 22 3/4 by 30 3/4 inches.

626. *Proa.* [Año I, no. 1-Año I, no. 2. Buenos Aires, August 1922-December 1922].

First series of *Proa.*

627. *Proa.* [Año I,] no. 1-[Año II,] no. 13. Buenos Aires, [August 1924-November 1925].

Literary journal devoted to the Ultraist movement, founded by Borges, Brandan Caraffa, Ricardo Güiraldes, and Pablo Rojas Paz. The journal also featured artwork by Norah Borges. This second series was preceded by one in August 1922, which lasted for only two issues. Borges contributed to all but no. 9 of this second series. Nos. 14 and 15, which complete the journal, are considered virtually impossible to find. No. 14 has recently been reprinted in facsimile, however.

628. *Proa (1924-1925).* Edición facsimilar de los números 1, 6, 8, 14. [Buenos Aires:] Centro Editor de América Latina, 1983.
[152 leaves, varying page numbers] 19 cm.
(Capítulo-La historia de la literatura argentina.)

Facsimile reprint of several rare issues of this journal, dating from August 1924 to December 1925. No. 14, in particular, is exceedingly scarce.

629. Reid, Alastair.

Weathering. Poems and Translations. [Edinburgh:] Canongate, [1978].
[i-x], [1-2] 3-125 [126] p. 22 cm.

Includes Reid's translations of poems by Borges and Pablo Neruda.

630. Silva Valdéz, Fernán.

"Ellos y nosotros. Poema familiar a Jorge Luis Borges." (In: *Proa*, Año II, no. 14, p. 15. Buenos Aires, December 1925).

631. *La vida literaria; crítica, información bibliográfica.* Año I, no. 1-Año V, no. 12 (43). Buenos Aires, July 1928-July 1932.

Complete collection of this rare periodical.

632. Villar, Amado.

Marimorena. 33 poemas. Buenos Aires: El Ateneo, 1934.
[1-6] 7-100 [101-104] p. 17.5 cm.

Copy owned by Borges. Contains author's inscription: "A/ Jorge Luis Borges,/ con entrañable admiración,/ y/ fraternal afecto.--/A. Villar/ s/c Franklin, 914.--/Bs. Aires.--julio de 1935."

XI. CRITICISM AND BIOGRAPHIES

633. Acevedo de Borges, Leonor.

"Propos de Mme. Leonor Acevedo de Borges." (In: *Cahiers de L'Herne*, no. 4, pp. 9-11. Paris, 1964).

Appears in "Des témoins" section. 3 copies.

634. Agheana, Ian T.

The Prose of Jorge Luis Borges: Existentialism and the Dynamics of Surprise. New York-Berne-Frankfort on the Main-Nancy: Peter Lang, [1984].
[1 unnumbered leaf], [i-vi] vii-xiii [xiv], [1] 2-320 p. 22.5 cm.
(American University Studies. Series II: Romance languages and literature, 13.)

635. Aizenberg, Edna.

The Aleph Weaver: Biblical, Kabbalistic and Judaic Elements in Borges. [Potomac, Md.:]
Scripta Humanistica, [1984].
[i-iv] v-x, [1-2] 3-164 [165-166] p. 22 cm.
(Scripta humanistica.)

636. Alazraki, Jaime.

"Borges and the Kabbalah." (In: *Tri Quarterly*, no. 25, pp. 240-267. Evanston, Ill., Fall 1972).

637. Alazraki, Jaime.

"Borges and the New Latin-American Novel." (In: *Tri Quarterly*, no. 25, pp. 379-398. Evanston, Ill., Fall 1972).

Preceded by a photograph of the Café Victoria in Buenos Aires, on p. 378.

638. Alazraki, Jaime.

Jorge Luis Borges. Edición de Jaime Alazraki.
[Madrid:] Taurus, [1976].
[1-8] 9-364 [365-368] p. 21 cm.
(Serie el escritor y la crítica.)
(Persiles, 88.)

639. Alazraki, Jaime.

La prosa narrativa de Jorge Luis Borges; temas-estilo.
Madrid: Editorial Gredos, S.A., [1968].
[1-7] 8-246 [247-256] p. 20 cm.
(Biblioteca románica hispánica, II. Estudios y ensayos, 112.)

2 copies.

BECCO 320

640. Alazraki, Jaime.

La prosa narrativa de Jorge Luis Borges; temas-estilo.
Madrid: Editorial Gredos, [1983].
[i-ii], [1-5] 6-489 [490] p. 19.5 cm.
(Biblioteca románica hispánica, II. Estudios y ensayos, 112.)

Third edition.

[BECCO 320]

641. Alazraki, Jaime.

Versiones. Inversiones. Reversiones. El espejo como modelo estructural del relato en dos cuentos de Borges. [Madrid:] Editorial Gredos, [1977].
[1-9] 10-156 [157-176] p. 19 cm.
(Biblioteca románica hispánica, VII. Campo abierto, 36.)

2 copies.

642. Albano, Mario.

“Atisbo de interpretación argentina: Jorge Luis Borges.” (In: *Sur*, Año XVI, no. 169, pp. 61-64. Buenos Aires, November 1948).

Article appearing in “Crónicas” section.

BECCO 328

643. Alfieri, Teresa.

Redes, alambiques y herencias. [Buenos Aires:] Editorial de Belgrano, [1981].
[1-9] 10-189 [190-192] p. 20 cm.

Includes chapter entitled “La repercusión de Borges en Francia,” pp. [15]-105.

644. Alter, Robert.

“Borges and Stevens: A Note on Post-Symbolist Writing.” (In: *Tri Quarterly*, no. 25, pp. 323-333. Evanston, Ill., Fall 1972).

645. André, Robert.

“La mort vécue de J. L. Borges.” (In: *Cahiers de L’Herne*, no. 4, pp. 328-333. Paris, 1964).

Appears in “Essais” section. 3 copies.

BECCO 359

646. Antezana Juárez, Luis H.

Algebra y fuego: lectura de Borges. Louvain, Editions Nauwelaerts, 1978.
[i-vii] viii-xvi, [1] 2-163 [164] p. 25 cm.
(Université de Louvain. Recueil de travaux d’histoire et de philologie: 6e série, Fascicule 13.)

647. Antunes, Nara Maia.

Jogo de espelhos (Borges e a teoria da literatura). Rio de Janeiro: Livraria José Olympio Editora, 1982.
[i-viii], 1-167 [168] p. 21 cm.

648. Appratto, Roberto.

Jorge Luis Borges. Aspectos de su narrativa y de su poesía. Montevideo: Editorial Técnica S.R.L., 1979.
[1-3] 4-55 [56-60] p. 21 cm.
(Manuales de literatura, 58.)

649. Arfini, Alfredo.

Borges: pobre ciego balbuciente. Rosario: Librería y Editorial Ruíz, 1968.
[1-2] 3-11 [12] p. 17 cm.

2 copies.

BECCO 398

650. *Asedio a Jorge Luis Borges*. Edición de Joaquín Marco. [Madrid:] Ultramar, [1982, c. 1981].
[1-8] 9-261 [262-264] p. 21 cm.
(Serie azul.)

First Spanish-language edition.

651. Bajarlía, Juan-Jacobo.

La polémica Reverdy-Huidobro. Origen del ultraísmo. Prefacio de Fernand Verhesen. Buenos Aires: Editorial Devenir, 1964.
[1-6] 7-59 [60-64] p. 20 cm.
(Colección el cuadrante.)

Includes discussion of Borges and early Ultraism.

652. Barnatán, Marcos Ricardo.

Conocer Borges y su obra. [Barcelona:] Dopesa, [1978].
[1-10] 11-125 [126-128] p. 18.5 cm.
(Colección conocer, 10.)

653. Barnatán, Marcos Ricardo.

Jorge Luis Borges. [Madrid:] Ediciones Júcar, [1972].
[1-10] 11-211 [212-216] p. 18.5 cm.
(Colección los poetas, 2.)

BECCO 424

654. Barrenechea, Ana María.

Borges the Labyrinth Maker. Edited and translated by Robert Lima. [New York:] New York University Press, 1965.
[i-vi] vii-x [xi-xii], 1-175 [176-180] p. 21 cm.
(The Gotham library.)

Gift of Joan St. C. Crane.

BECCO 434

655. Barrenechea, Ana María.

La expresión de la irrealidad en la obra de Jorge Luis Borges. [México:] El Colegio de México, 1957.
[1-8] 9-189 [190-192] p. 21.5 cm.

First edition. 2 copies.

BECCO 432

656. Barrenechea, Ana María.

La expresión de la irrealidad en la obra de Jorge Luis Borges. [Buenos Aires:] Paidós, [1967].

[1-8] 9-270 [271-272] p. 18.5 cm.

(Letras argentinas Paidós, 5.)

2 copies.

BECCO 435

657. Barrenechea, Ana María.

"Une fiction de Jorge Luis Borges." (In: *Cahiers de L'Herne*, no. 4, pp. 309-311. Paris, 1964).

Appears in "Essais" section. 3 copies.

BECCO 433

658. Barros, Jenny.

"Borges": su estilo narrativo. [Montevideo:] Ediciones de la Casa del Estudiante, [1978].
[1-2] 3-83 [84-88] p. 19.5 cm.

659. Bastos, María Luisa.

Borges ante la crítica argentina, 1923-1960. Buenos Aires: Ediciones Hispamérica, [1974].
[3-10] 11-356 [357-358] p. 20 cm.

Lacks pp. [1-2] (blank). This leaf is missing in both copies, which may indicate that the normal pagination is as shown. 2 copies.

660. *Begegnung mit Borges.* [München:] Hanser, [1983].
8 unnumbered leaves [pp. 1-16]. 22.5 cm.
(Bogen, 8.)

661. Belitt, Ben.

"The Enigmatic Predicament: Some Parables of Kafka and Borges." (In: *Tri Quarterly*, no. 25, pp. 268-293. Evanston, Ill., Fall 1972).

662. Bénichou, Paul.

"Koublai Khan, Coleridge et Borges." (In: *Cahiers de L'Herne*, no. 4, pp. 365-368).

Appears in "Essais" section. 3 copies.

BECCO 453

663. Bensoussan, Albert.

"Borges: Le mystère du nom." (In: *Europe*, no. 637, pp. [121]-125. Paris, May 1982).

664. Bernard, Michel.

"Le bon usage." (In: *Cahiers de L'Herne*, no. 4, pp. 115-116. Paris, 1964).

Appears in "Interférences" section. 3 copies.

BECCO 456

665. Bernès, Jean-Pierre A.

"Cortes y Quebradas. Borges généalogiste du tango." (In: *Europe*, no. 637, pp. [84]-91. Paris, May 1982).

666. Berveiller, Michel.

Le cosmopolitisme de Jorge Luis Borges. [Paris: Didier, 1973].

[1-9] 10-507 [508-512] p. 24 cm.
(Publications de la Sorbonne. Série littératures, 4.)

667. Bianco, José.

"Des souvenirs." (In: *Cahiers de L'Herne*, no. 4, pp. 33-43. Paris, 1964).

Appears in "Des témoins" section. 3 copies.

BECCO 463

668. Bioy Casares, Adolfo.

"Lettres et amitiés." (In: *Cahiers de L'Herne*, no. 4, pp. 12-18. Paris, 1964).

Appears in "Des témoins" section. 3 copies.

669. Bloom, Harold.

"Richard Burgin: *Conversations with Jorge Luis Borges*." (In: *Review '69*, pp. 60-62. New York, 1970).

670. Blume, Jaime.

Un prólogo y tres autores. [Santiago:] Ediciones Aconcagua, [1977].
[1-10] 11-258 [259-260] p. 18 cm.
(Colección Bello.)

Critical essays on Borges, García Lorca, and Gabriela Mistral.

671. Borello, Rodolfo A.

"La narrativa fantástica: Borges." (In: *Capítulo, la historia de la literatura argentina*, no. 48, pp. 1129-1152. Buenos Aires, 1968).

672. *Borges.* [Buenos Aires:] Editorial El Mangrullo S.A., [1976].
[1-2] 3-94 [95-96] p. 18 cm.
(Colección letra abierta, 1.)

673. "Borges and the Madrid of 1920." (In: *Spain 85*, Year XIII, no. 144, p. [12]. Madrid, July 1985).

674. *Borges, Bulatovic, Canetti.* Drei Gesprache mit Horst Bienek. [München:] Carl Hanser Verlag, [1965].
[1-4] 5-40 [41-44] p. 20.5 cm.

675. *Borges: obra y personaje.* Washington Benavides, Martha Canfield, Roberto de Espada, Milton Forraro, Guillermo Sucre. Montevideo: Acali Editorial, 1978.
[1-4] 5-119 [120-128] p. 19.5 cm.
(Colección estudios críticos, 2.)

3 copies. One copy, gift of C. Jared Loewenstein.

676. *Borges, oral. El libro, la inmortalidad, Emanuel Swedenborg, el cuento policial, el tiempo.* [Buenos Aires:] Emecé Editores/Editorial de Belgrano, [1979].
[1-6] 7-108 [109-112] p. 22 cm.

677. *Borges para millones.* [Buenos Aires:] Corregidor, [1978].
[1-6] 7-111 [112] p. 22.5 cm.

This text was used as a source for the film on Borges made under the same title.

678. *Borges, the Poet. A Symposium on the Poetry of Jorge Luis Borges.* Carlisle, Pa.: Dickinson College, 1983.
1-24 p. 28 cm.

Program for the Borges symposium held at Dickinson College, April 6-8, 1983. Gift of Linda S. Maier.

679. *Borges y la crítica. Antología.* Ana M. Barrenechea, Jaime Rest, John Updike y otros. [Buenos Aires:] Centro Editor de América Latina, [1981].
[1-6], i-iv, 7-106 [107-108] p. 18 cm.
(Capítulo. Biblioteca argentina fundamental, 80.)

680. Bottone, Mireya.

La literatura argentina y el cine. Santa Fe: Universidad Nacional del Litoral, [1964].
[1-3] 4-36 [37-52] p. 23 cm.
(Cuadernos del Instituto de Letras. Facultad de Filosofía y Letras.)

Mentions film version of Borges' "Emma Zunz," made in 1954 under the title "Días de odio."

681. Boyles, Yolanda Julia.

The German Response to Latin American Literature and the Reception of Jorge Luis Borges and Pablo Neruda. Heidelberg: Carl Winter Universitätsverlag, 1981.
[1-5] 6-303 [304] p. 22 cm.
(Reihe Siegen, 31.)

682. Braceli, Rodolfo E.

"Borges deux fois aveugle." (In: *Europe*, no. 637, pp. [108]-114. Paris, May 1982).

683. Braceli, Rodolfo E.

Don Borges, saque su cuchillo porque he venido a matarlo. [Buenos Aires:] Editorial Galerna, [1979]. [3-8] 9-189 [190-194] p. 18 cm.

684. Brion, Marcel.

"Masques, miroirs, monsonges et labyrinthe." (In: *Cahiers de L'Herne*, no. 4, pp. 312-322. Paris, 1964).

Appears in "Essais" section. 3 copies.

BECCO 503

685. Caillois, Roger.

"Les thèmes fondamentaux de J. L. Borges." (In: *Cahiers de L'Herne*, no. 4, pp. 211-217. Paris, 1964).

Appears in "Essais" section. 3 copies.

BECCO 514

686. Calaf de Aguera, Helen.

"El doble en el tiempo en 'El otro' de Jorge L. Borges." (In: *Explicación de textos literarios*, Vol. VI, no. 2, pp. 167-173. Sacramento, 1978).

687. Campo, Cristina.

"La porte magique." (In: *Cahiers de L'Herne*, no. 4, pp. 113-114. Paris, 1964).

Appears in "Interférences" section. 3 copies.

BECCO 517

688. Cansinos-Assens, Rafael.

"Evocation de Jorge Luis Borges." (In: *Cahiers de L'Herne*, no. 4, p. 7. Paris, 1964).

Appears in "Des témoins" section. 3 copies.

BECCO 525

689. Canto, Estela.

"Jorge Luis Borges: 'El Aleph'." (In: *Sur*, Año XVII, no. 180, pp. 93-98. Buenos Aires, October 1949).

BECCO 527

690. Cantonnet, María Ester.

Hombre, tiempo y espacio en la narrativa de Pedro Leandro Ipuche y Jorge Luis Borges. [Montevideo:] Ediciones de la Banda Oriental, [1984].
[i-ii], [1-9] 10-99 [100] p. 18.5 cm.

691. Cantonnet, María Ester.

Hombre, tiempo y espacio en la temática de Jorge Luis Borges y Pedro Leandro Ipuche. [Montevideo: Centro Interdisciplinario de Estudios sobre el Desarollo Uruguay, 1982].
[i-iii], 1-133 p. (recto only) 28 cm.

692. Capouya, Emile.

"Jorge Luis Borges: *Other Inquisitions, 1937-1952.*" (In: *Review '68*, pp. 35-37. New York, 1969).

693. *The Cardinal Points of Borges.* Edited by Lowell Dunham and Ivar Ivask. Norman: University of Oklahoma Press, [1971].

[i-iv] v-ix [x], [1] 2-113 [114-118] p. 26 cm.

Some of the articles were presented at the International Symposium on Borges, held at the University of Oklahoma, Dec. 5-6, 1969, and were first published in the Summer 1971 issue of *Books Abroad.*

BECCO 631

694. *The Cardinal Points of Borges.* Edited by Lowell Dunham and Ivar Ivask. Norman: University of Oklahoma Press, [1973, c. 1971].
[i-iv] v-ix [x], [1] 2-113 [114-118] p. 25.5 cm.

Second printing. Gift of Joan St. C. Crane.

[BECCO 631]

695. Carilla, Emilio.

Un cuento de Borges. Separata del Homenaje a Dámaso Alonso, Tomo I. Madrid: Editorial Gredos, 1960.
[i-ii], 1-12 p. 24 cm.

Offprint, pages 295-306 of *Homenaje a Dámaso Alonso.* Discussion of Borges' *La casa de Asterión.*

BECCO 537

696. Carilla, Emilio.

Estudios de literatura argentina (siglo XX). Tucumán: Universidad Nacional de Tucumán. Facultad de Filosofía y Letras, 1968.
[1-6] 7-173 [174-176] p. 23 cm.
(Cuadernos de humanitas, 25.)

Includes chapter "Un cuento de Borges." Second edition.

[BECCO 538]

697. Carilla, Emilio.

Literatura argentina, 1800-1950 (esquema generacional). [Tucumán:] Ministerio de Educación de la Nación. Universidad Nacional de Tucumán. Facultad de Filosofía y Letras, [1954]. [1-4] 5-92 [93-96] p. 22.5 cm.
(Cuaderno de letras, 1.) (Universidad Nacional de Tucumán. Publicación, 662.)

698. Carrouges, Michel.

"Borges citoyen de Tlon." (In: *Cahiers de L'Herne*, no. 4, pp. 242-244. Paris, 1964).

Appears in "Essais" section. 3 copies.

BECCO 548

699. Cassou, Jean.

"L'exercice problématique de la littérature." (In: *Cahiers de L'Herne*, no. 4, pp. 106-108. Paris, 1964).

Appears in "Interférences" section. 3 copies.

BECCO 554

700. Castelli, Ferdinando.

I cavalieri del nulla. [Milano:] Massimo, [1977]. [1-4] 5-303 [304] p. 19.5 cm.

Includes biographical and critical studies of Borges, Pirandello, Faulkner, Hemingway, Beckett, and others. Each author is also represented by a selection from his works.

701. Castillo, Abelardo.

"Borges et la nouvelle génération." (In: *Cahiers de L'Herne*, no. 4, pp. 199-204. Paris, 1964).

Appears in "Situation" section. 3 copies.

BECCO 556

702. Childress, Mark.

"The Dark Riddle of Jorge Luis Borges." (In: *Saturday Review*, Vol. 9, no. 7, pp. 32-34. Columbia, Missouri, March-April 1983).

Joint author: Charles C. McNair, Jr. Interview with Borges.

703. Christ, Ronald J.

"Borges Justified: Notes and Texts toward Stations of a Theme." (In: *Tri Quarterly*, no. 25, pp. 52-87. Evanston, Ill., Fall 1972).

704. Christ, Ronald J.

The Narrow Act: Borges' Art of Allusion. New York: New York University Press/ London: University of London Press Limited, 1969. [i-viii] ix-xvi [xvii-xx], 1-244 p. 23.5 cm. (New York University studies in comparative literature, 2.)

BECCO 593

705. Citati, Piétro.

"L'imparfait bibliothécaire." (In: *Cahiers de L'Herne*, no. 4, pp. 272-275. Paris, 1964).

Appears in "Essais" section. 3 copies.

BECCO 563

706. Cócaro, Nicolás.

"Borges et les versions du courage." (In: *Cahiers de L'Herne*, no. 4, pp. 196-198. Paris, 1964).

Appears in "Situation" section. 3 copies.

BECCO 567

707. Cócaro, Nicolás.

Las manos de Borges. Buenos Aires: Francisco A. Colombo, [1966].
8 unnumbered leaves [pp. 1-16]. 29.5 cm.

Drawings by Elbio Fernández. Brief sketches of Borges written by eleven authors, including Cócaro, Manuel Mújica Laínez, and others.

BECCO 1374

708. Coleman, Alexander.

"Chaos and Play in Borges." (In: *Círculo: revista de cultura*, Vol. VI, pp. 27-33. Verona, N.J., 1977).

709. Coleman, Alexander.

"Introductory Note." (In: *Review '69*, pp. 7-10. New York, 1970).

710. Coleman, Alexander.

"Notes on Borges and American Literature." (In: *Tri Quarterly*, no. 25, pp. 356-377. Evanston, Ill., Fall 1972).

711. *Contra Borges*. Compilación y estudio preliminar de Juan Fló. [Buenos Aires:] Editorial Galerna, [1978].

[1-6] 7-196 [197-200] p. 19 cm.
(Colección polemos, 3.)

712. Cortanze, Gérard de.

"Chronologie de Jorge Luis Borges." (In: *Europe*, no. 637, pp. [142]-153. Paris, May 1982).

713. Cortanze, Gérard de.

"Stranger in the Night." (In: *Europe*, no. 637, pp. [6]-12. Paris, May 1982).

714. Corvalán, Octavio.

La letra en el espejo (*ensayos*). Salta, Argentina: Universidad Nacional de Salta, Dpto. de Humanidades, 1982.
[1-7] 8-111 [112-116] p. 21.5 cm.

Contains three essays on Borges.

715. Covizzi, Lenira Marques.

O insólito em Guimarães Rosa e Borges. (Crise da Mimese/ Mimese da crise). São Paulo, Editora Atica, 1978.
[1-15] 16-156 [157-160] p. 21 cm.
(Ensaios, 49.)

716. Cowes, Hugo.

La creación de Dulcinea y la referencia literaria. (*Sobre Jorge Luis Borges, autor del Quijote*). [Buenos Aires:] Libros de Hispanoamérica, [1984].
[1-2] 3-15 [16] p. 21.5 cm.

717. Coyné, André.

"Une littérature du 'soupçon'." (In: *Cahiers de L'Herne*, no. 4, pp. 334-342. Paris, 1964).

Appears in "Essais" section. 3 copies.

BECCO 585

718. Cozarinsky, Edgardo.

Borges en/y/sobre el cine. [Madrid: Editorial Fundamentos, 1981].
[1-6] 7-148 [149-160] p. 20.5 cm.
(Colección espiral/ ensayo, 60.)

719. Cozarinsky, Edgardo.

Borges y el cine. Buenos Aires: Sur, [1974].
[1-7] 8-134 [135-136] p. 20 cm.

2 copies.

720. "40 inquisiciones sobre Borges." (In: *Revista iberoamericana*, nos. 100-101, pp. [i-xiv], [257] 258-756 [757-798]. México, July-December 1977).

Special number dedicated to Borges. Contains articles on Borges by a variety of literary critics and historians. Edited by Alfredo A. Roggiano and Emir Rodríguez Monegal.

721. Daireaux, Max.

Panorama de la littérature hispano-américaine.
Paris: Editions Kra, [1930].
[1-8] 9-314 [315-316] p. 19 cm.
(Collection des panoramas des littératures contemporaines.)

Contains a brief biography of José [sic] Luis Borges, and states: "Né en 1900 (sic), il est le chef de l'ultraisme argentin." This copy inscribed by author: "A Nicolas Coronado/sincero homenaje/ Max Daireaux."

722. Damade, Jacques.

"Le Dieu indifférent et le voyageur immobile." (In: *Europe*, no. 637, pp. [126]-130. Paris, May 1982).

723. Damade, Jacques.

"J. L. B.: une nécrologie." (In: *Europe*, no. 637, pp. [139]-140. Paris, May 1982).

724. Day, Douglas.

"Borges, Faulkner, and *The Wild Palms*." (In: *The Virginia Quarterly Review*, Vol. 56, no. 1, pp. 109-118. Charlottesville, Winter 1980).

725. De Mott, Benjamin.

"Jorge Luis Borges: *The Book of Imaginary Beings*." (In: *Review '69*, pp. 43-45. New York, 1970).

726. *Des témoins, correspondance, inédits, interférences, situations, essais, "Borges et Borges," chronologie de l'ultraisme, biographie, glossaire argentin, bibliographie, iconographie*. [Paris:] L'Herne, [1964].
[i-x], [1-6] 7-516 [517-538] p. 27 cm.
(Cahiers de L'Herne, 4.)

3 copies. Individual articles appearing in this source are cited separately in the present bibliographic text.

727. "Desagravio a Borges." (In: *Sur*, Año XII, no. 94, pp. [7]-34. Buenos Aires, July 1942).

Segments written by 21 authors, including Eduardo Mallea, Luis Emilio Soto, Pedro Henríquez Ureña, Amado Alonso, Eduardo González Lanuza, Gloria Alcorta, Adolfo Bioy Casares, José Bianco, Carlos Mastronardi, Enrique Amorim, Ernesto Sábato, and others.

BECCO 606

728. Devoto, Daniel.

"Aleph et Alexis." (In: *Cahiers de L'Herne*, no. 4, pp. 280-292. Paris, 1964).

Appears in "Essais" section. 3 copies.

BECCO 608

729. Domínguez Morillo, Rocío.

"Borges . . . creador de cielos y negador de dioses." (In: *Pájaro de fuego*, Año I, no. 6, p. 50. Buenos Aires, April-May 1978).

730. Doreste, Ventura.

"Analyse de Borges." (In: *Cahiers de L'Herne*, no. 4, pp. 228-236. Paris, 1964).

Appears in "Essais" section. 3 copies.

BECCO 620

731. Drieu la Rochelle, Pierre.

"Borges vaut le voyage." (In: *Cahiers de L'Herne*, no. 4, p. 105. Paris, 1964).

Appears in "Interférences" section. 3 copies.

BECCO 624

732. Dujovne-Ortiz, Alicia.

"Borges et l'effroyable sphère." (In: *Europe*, no. 637, pp. [77]-83. Paris, May 1982).

733. Durán, Manuel.

"Les deux Borges." (In: *Cahiers de L'Herne*, no. 4, pp. 237-241. Paris, 1964).

Appears in "Essais" section. 3 copies.

BECCO 633

734. Durand, René L. F.

"L'hommage de Borges à Dakar." (In: *Cahiers de L'Herne*, no. 4, pp. 362-364. Paris, 1964).

Appears in "Essais" section. 3 copies.

BECCO 636

735. Enguídanos, Miguel.

"Le caractère argentin de Borges." (In: *Cahiers de L'Herne*, no. 4, pp. 129-136. Paris, 1964).

Appears in "Situation" section. 3 copies.

BECCO 648

736. "El escritor y el hombre." (In: *Clarín: cultura y nación*, p. 3. Buenos Aires, 23 August 1979).

Critical analysis of Borges' works by Ernesto Sábato and others. Gift of C. Jared Loewenstein.

737. Etchebarne, Miguel D.

La influencia del arrabal en la poesia argentina culta. Buenos Aires: Editorial Guillermo Kraft Limitada, [1955].
[1-7] 8-194 [195-200] p. 20.5 cm.
(Colección cúpula.)

738. *Expliquémonos a Borges como poeta.* Compilación y prólogo de Angel Flores. [México:] Siglo Veintiuno Editores, [1984].
[1-4] 5-309 [310-312] p. 18 cm.
(La creación literaria.)

739. Fens, Kees.

"Gebed om een goed einde." (In: *New Found Land,* Jaargang I, no. 1, pp. 44-45. Amsterdam, September 1981).

Critical notes on Borges' poem "El ángel."

740. Fernández, Ariel.

Tres en la literatura de nuestra América: Borges, Vargas Llosa, Campos Menéndez. Santiago: Ediciones Tamarugal, [1984].
[1-6] 7-90 [91-92] p. 19 cm.

741. Fernández Moreno, César.

"Chronologie de l'ultraisme." (In: *Cahiers de L'Herne*, no. 4, pp. 469-475. Paris, 1964).

3 copies.

[BECCO 672]

742. Fernández Moreno, César.

"Dos destinos." (In: *Testigo,* no. 3, pp. 31-35. Buenos Aires, July-September 1966).

Article subtitled "El ultraísmo" and "Borges."

BECCO 674

743. Fernández Moreno, César.

Esquema de Borges. Buenos Aires: Editorial Perrot, [1957].
[1-8] 9-65 [66-68] p. 18.5 cm.
(Colección nuevo mundo, 9.)

2 copies.

BECCO 672

744. Fields, Kenneth.

"Business from Porlock." (In: *Tri Quarterly,* no. 25, pp. 231-239. Evanston, Ill., Fall 1972).

A prose essay by the poet Fields, done in Borgesian style. Makes comparisons to Borges' texts.

745. Fresán, Juan.

BioAutoBiografía de Jorge Luis Borges. [Buenos Aires:] Siglo XXI Editores, [1970].
72 unnumbered leaves [pp. 1-144]. 21.5 cm.

First edition. 2 copies.

BECCO 699

746. Garayalde, Giovanna de.

Jorge Luis Borges: Sources and Illumination. London: The Octagon Press, [1978].
[1-6] 7-88 p. 22 cm.

747. García Márquez, Eligio.

Son así. Reportaje a nueve escritores latinoamericanos. [Bogotá:] Editorial La Oveja Negra, [1982].
[1-6] 7-231 [232] p. 19.5 cm.

The brother of Gabriel García Márquez discusses "Jorge Luis Borges: la alucinación dirigida," pp. [11]-24.

748. García Pinto, R.

"Un poema de Borges." (In: *Sur*, no. 253, pp. 69-71. Buenos Aires, July-August 1958).

BECCO 707

749. Garcia Ponce, Juan.

La errancia sin fin: Musil, Borges, Klossowski. Barcelona: Editorial Anagrama, [1981].
[1-8] 9-85 [86-88] p. 20 cm.
(Colección argumentos, 63.)

750. Garramuño, Carlos A.

"La vigilia con los ojos abiertos. Encuentro con Borges." (In: *Pájaro de fuego*, Año I, no. 6, pp. [39]-49. Buenos Aires, April-May 1978).

751. Gass, William H.

"Jorge Luis Borges: *The Book of Imaginary Beings*; Richard Burgin: *Conversations with Jorge Luis Borges*; Ronald Christ: *The Narrow Act: Borges' Art of Allusion*." (In: *Review '69*, pp. 27-36. New York, 1970).

752. Genette, Gérard.

"La littérature selon Borges." (In: *Cahiers de L'Herne*, no. 4, pp. 323-327. Paris, 1964).

Appears in "Essais" section. 3 copies.

BECCO 712

753. Genot, Gérard.

Jorge Luis Borges. Firenze: La Nuova Italia, 1974.
1-168 [169-172] p. 16.5 cm.
(Il castoro, 31-32).

754. Gertel, Zunilda.

Borges y su retorno a la poesía. New York: The University of Iowa/ Las Américas Publishing Company, [1969, c. 1967].
[1-13] 14-174 [175-176] p. 21.5 cm.

BECCO 718

755. Ghiano, Juan Carlos.

"Boedo y Florida." (In: *Ficción*, no. 7, pp. 135-140. Buenos Aires, May-June 1957).

Article appearing in "Letras argentinas" section.

756. Ghiano, Juan Carlos.

Temas y aptitudes. (Lugones, Güiraldes, Quiroga, Arlt, Marechal, Bernárdez, Borges, Molina). [Buenos Aires:] Ollantay, [1949].
[1-6] 7-83 [84-88] p. 20 cm.
(Colección "cuatro vientos". Serie ensayo, 4.)

BECCO 722

757. Gobello, José.

Las letras del tango de Villoldo a Borges. [Buenos Aires:] Stilman Editores, [1979].
[1-6] 7-156 [157-160] p. 18 cm.

758. Goloboff, Gerardo Mario.

Leer Borges. [Buenos Aires: Editorial Huemul, 1978].
[1-10] 11-348 [349-352] p. 17.5 cm.
(Colección temas del hombre, 18.)

759. Goloboff, Gerardo Mario.

"Moi, malheureusement, je sui Borges." (In: *Europe*, no. 637, pp. [24]-33. Paris, May 1982).

760. Gomes, Manuel João.

Almanaque dos espelhos. Variaçoes narcísicas sobre temas de Ovídio, Hoffmann, Chamisso, Ricardo Reis, Lewis Carroll, Alvaro de Campos, Nerval, Wenceslau de Moraes, Borges e Maupassant. [Lisboa: Publicações Culturais Engrenagem, Lda., 1980].
[1-9] 10-55 [56-58] p. 17.5 cm.
(& etc.)

761. Grünberg, Carlos M.

"Jorge Luis Borges: *El idioma de los argentinos*." (In: *La vida literaria; crítica, información bibliográfica*, Año I, no. 11, p. 5. Buenos Aires, June 1929).

Review appearing in "Crítica de libros" section.

762. Guardi, Mario Bernardi.

L'io plurale: Borges et Borges. In appendice scritti e testimonianze di Fausto Gianfraceschi, Francesco Tentori Montalto, Roberto Paoli, Claudio Quarantotto, Marcello Staglieno. Milano: Società Editrice Il Falco, 1979.
[1-12] 13-170 [171-180] p. 21 cm.
(Collana "Il ponte", 4.)

Copy number 1,230 of 3,000.

763. Gutiérrez Girardot, Rafael.

"Borges el hacedor." (In: *Cahiers de L'Herne*, no. 4, pp. 245-251. Paris, 1964).

Appears in "Essais" section. 3 copies.

BECCO 781

764. Gutiérrez Girardot, Rafael.

"Borges en Allemagne." (In: *Cahiers de L'Herne*, no. 4, pp. 205-208. Paris, 1964).

Appears in "Situation" section. 3 copies.

BECCO 780

765. Gutiérrez Girardot, Rafael.

Jorge Luis Borges. Ensayo de interpretación. Madrid: "Insula," 1959.
[1-6] 7-139 [140] p. 21.5 cm.

At head of title: Instituto Ibero-Americano Gotemburgo Suecia. 2 copies.

BECCO 776

766. Hall, Remy Inglis.

"Richard Burgin: *Conversations with Jorge Luis Borges.*" (In: *Review '69*, pp. 62-64. New York, 1970).

767. Harss, Luis.

Into the Mainstream. Conversations with Latin-American Writers. New York: Harper & Row, Publishers, [1967].
[i-viii], 1-385 [386-390] p. 22 cm.

First edition. Joint author: Barbara Dohmann. Includes critical essays on Borges, Carpentier, Asturias, Onetti, Cortázar, Fuentes, García Márquez, and Vargas Llosa.

BECCO 785

768. Harss, Luis.

Los nuestros. Luis Harss en colaboración con Barbara Dohmann. Buenos Aires: Editorial Sudamericana, [1966].
[1-9] 10-461 [462-464] p. 19.5 cm.

Spanish translation of: *Into the Mainstream.* Critical essays on contemporary Latin American fiction writers, including Borges.

BECCO 786

769. Heidenry, John.

"Richard Burgin: *Conversations with Jorge Luis Borges*; Ronald Christ: *The Narrow Act: Borges' Art of Allusion*." (In: *Review '69*, pp. 37-38. New York, 1970).

770. Hoffman, Stanton.

"Jorge Luis Borges: *The Book of Imaginary Beings*." (In: *Review '69*, pp. 45-48. New York, 1970).

771. Horst, Karl August.

"Intentions et hasard dans l'oeuvre de Borges." (In: *Cahiers de L'Herne*, no. 4, pp. 218-223. Paris, 1964).

Appears in "Essais" section. 3 copies.

BECCO 799

772. Howard, Richard.

"Prose for Borges." (In: *Tri Quarterly*, no. 25, pp. 9-10. Evanston, Ill., Fall 1972).

773. Ibarra, Néstor.

"Borges et Borges." (In: *Cahiers de L'Herne*, no. 4, pp. [415]-465. Paris, 1964).

3 copies.

BECCO 806

774. Ibarra, Néstor.

"From 'Borges et Borges': The Final Dialogues." (In: *Tri Quarterly*, no. 25, pp. 88-99. Evanston, Ill., Fall 1972).

775. Ibarra, Néstor.

"Jorge Luis Borges, poeta." (In: *Síntesis*, Año III, no. 34, pp. 11-32. Buenos Aires, March 1930).

BECCO 802

776. Ibarra, Néstor.

La nueva poesía argentina; ensayo crítico sobre el ultraísmo, 1921-1929. Buenos Aires: Imp. Vda. de Molinari e Hijos, 1930.
[1-7] 8-132 [133-136] p. 19 cm.

Includes study of Borges' *Fervor de Buenos Aires, Luna de enfrente*, and *Cuaderno San Martín.*

BECCO 803

777. Isaacson, José.

Macedonio Fernández, sus ideas políticas y estéticas. [Buenos Aires:] Editorial de Belgrano, [1981].
[1-11] 12-125 [126-128] p. 20 cm.
(Colección figuras contemporáneas.)

Discussion in chapter 7 of "Macedonio, maestro de Borges."

778. Jitrik, Noé.

El fuego de la especie; ensayos sobre seis escritores argentinos. [Buenos Aires:] Siglo Veintiuno Argentina Editores, S.A. [1971].
[1-13] 14-188 [189-192] p. 18 cm.
(Crítica literaria.)

BECCO 834

779. *Jorge Luis Borges.* Pierre Macherey, Roger Caillois, Didier Anzieu, Carl August Horst, Maurice Jean Lefebre, Michel Carrouges, Louis Vax, Marcel Brion, Gérard Genette, Robert André, André Coyné. Buenos Aires: Editorial Freeland, 1978. [1-4] 5-157 [158-160] p. 19.5 cm.

780. "Jorge Luis Borges: *A Personal Anthology*." (In: *Review '68*, pp. 37-38. New York, 1969).

Originally published in *Time*, 24 March 1967.

781. "Jorge Luis Borges: *The Book of Imaginary Beings*." (In: *Review '69*, pp. 50-52. New York, 1970).

Originally published in *The New Republic*, 6 December 1969.

782. "Jorge Luis Borges: *The Book of Imaginary Beings*." (In: *Review '69*, pp. 57-60. New York, 1970).

Originally published in *Time*, 5 January 1970.

783. Juarroz, Roberto.

"Adrogué, Borges et les périphéries." (In: *Cahiers de L'Herne*, no. 4, pp. 194-195. Paris, 1964).

Appears in "Situation" section. 3 copies.

BECCO 836

784. Jurado, Alicia.

"Borges professeur de littérature." (In: *Cahiers de L'Herne*, no. 4, pp. 44-47. Paris, 1964).

Appears in "Des témoins" section. 3 copies.

BECCO 840

785. Jurado, Alicia.

Genio y figura de Jorge Luis Borges. [Buenos Aires:] Editorial Universitaria de Buenos Aires, [1964].
[1-4] 5-189 [190-192] p. 18 cm.
(Biblioteca de América. Colección genio y figura, 2.)

First edition.

BECCO 839

786. Jurado, Alicia.

Genio y figura de Jorge Luis Borges. [Buenos Aires:] Editorial Universitaria de Buenos Aires, [1966].
[1-4] 5-191 [192] p. 18 cm.
(Biblioteca de América. Colección genio y figura, 2.)

Second edition.

[BECCO 839]

787. Jurado, Alicia.

Genio y figura de Jorge Luis Borges. [Buenos Aires:] Editorial Universitaria de Buenos Aires, [1980].
[1-8] 9-198 [199-200] p. 18 cm.
(Genio y figura, 2.)

Third edition.

[BECCO 839]

788. Justo, Liborio.

Literatura argentina y expresión americana. [Buenos Aires:] Editorial Rescate, [1977, c. 1976].
[1-6] 7-190 [191-192] p. 19.5 cm.

789. Kennedy, William.

"Richard Burgin: *Conversations with Jorge Luis Borges*; Ronald Christ: *The Narrow Act: Borges' Art of Allusion.*" (In: *Review '69*, pp. 39-40. New York, 1970).

790. Kenny, Herbert A.

"Richard Burgin: *Conversations with Jorge Luis Borges.*" (In: *Review '69*, pp. 64-65. New York, 1970).

791. Kerrigan, Anthony.

"Borges à Madrid." (In: *Cahiers de L'Herne*, no. 4, pp. 118-124. Paris, 1964).

Appears in "Interférences" section. 3 copies.

BECCO 845

792. Kerrigan, Anthony.

"Borges/Unamuno." (In: *Tri Quarterly*, no. 25, pp. 294-311. Evanston, Ill., Fall 1972).

793. Kinzie, Mary.

"Preface for Americans." (In: *Tri Quarterly*, no. 25, pp. 5-8. Evanston, Ill., Fall 1972).

Introductory essay on Borges for a special issue devoted to his works and criticism.

794. Kinzie, Mary.

"Recursive Prose." (In: *Tri Quarterly*, no. 25, pp. 11-51. Evanston, Ill., Fall 1972).

Analysis of the psychology of Averroes and other Borgesian characters.

795. Lange, Victor.

"Jorge Luis Borges: *A Personal Anthology*." (In: *Review '68*, pp. 40-43. New York, 1969).

796. Lapouge, Gilles.

"L'influence de Borges." (In: *Europe*, no. 637, pp. [103]-106. Paris, May 1982).

797. Larbaud, Valéry.

"Sur Borges." (In: *Cahiers de L'Herne*, no. 4, pp. 111-112. Paris, 1964).

Appears in "Interférences" section. 3 copies.

BECCO 861

798. Lefebre, Maurice-Jean.

"Qui a écrit Borges." (In: *Cahiers de L'Herne*, no. 4, pp. 224-227. Paris, 1964).

Appears in "Essais" section. 3 copies.

BECCO 866

799. Lehmann-Haupt, Christopher.

"Jorge Luis Borges: *The Book of Imaginary Beings*." (In: *Review '69*, pp. 48-50. New York, 1970).

800. Lemm, Robert.

"Hoe ik 'El ángel' lees." (In: *New Found Land*, Jaargang I, no. 1, p. 47. Amsterdam, September 1981.)

Commentary on Borges' poem "El ángel."

801. Leonard, John.

"Richard Burgin: *Conversations with Jorge Luis Borges*; Ronald Christ: *The Narrow Act: Borges' Art of Allusion*." (In: *Review '69*, pp. 41-42. New York, 1970).

802. Libertella, Hector.

"Borges, écriture = propriété = contrat." (In: *Europe*, no. 637, pp. [131]-137. Paris, May 1982).

803. Lida de Malkiel, María Rosa.

"Contribución al estudio de las fuentes literarias de Jorge Luis Borges." (In: *Sur*, no. 213-214, pp. [50]-57. Buenos Aires, July-August 1952).

BECCO 871

804. Lindstrom, Naomi.

Macedonio Fernández. [Lincoln, Neb.: Society of Spanish and Spanish-American Studies, 1981]. [1-8] 9-138 [139-144] p. 21.5 cm.

Includes a discussion of the involvement of Fernández with the Argentine literary vanguard of the 1920s. Borges, a member of that group, considered himself a disciple of Fernández.

805. Mac Shane, Frank.

"Borges the Craftsman." (In: *Tri Quarterly*, no. 25, pp. 399-402. Evanston, Ill., Fall 1972).

806. Magrini, César.

"Fondation mythologique de Borges." (In: *Cahiers de L'Herne*, no. 4, pp. 185-193. Paris, 1964).

Appears in "Situation" section. 3 copies.

BECCO 903

807. Maloff, Saul.

"Jorge Luis Borges: *A Personal Anthology*." (In: *Review '68*, pp. 38-40. New York, 1969).

808. Marcel d'Ans, André.

"Jorge Luis Borges et la poésie d'Amérique." (In: *Cahiers de L'Herne*, no. 4, pp. 144-150. Paris, 1964).

Appears in "Situation" section. 3 copies.

BECCO 911

809. Marcenac, Jean.

"Borges." (In: *Europe*, no. 637, pp. [3]-5. Paris, May 1982).

810. Marchison, John C.

"The Greater Voice: On the Poetry of Jorge Luis Borges." (In: *Tri Quarterly*, no. 25, pp. 312-322. Evanston, Ill., Fall 1972).

811. Massuh, Gabriela.

Borges: Eine Asthetik des Schweigens. Erlangen: Verlag Palm & Enke, 1979.
[3 unnumbered leaves], i-ii, 1-235 [236-240] p. 21 cm.
(Erlanger Studien, 25.)

812. Massuh, Gabriela.

Borges: una estética del silencio. [Buenos Aires:] Editorial de Belgrano, [1980].
[1-8] 9-269 [270-272] p. 20 cm.
(Colección ensayos.)

813. Mastronardi, Carlos.

"B. Suárez Lynch: *'Un modelo para la muerte'*." (In: *Sur*, Año XV, no. 146, pp. 96-99. Buenos Aires, December 1946).

Article appearing in "Notas" section, under heading "Libros."

BECCO 920

814. Matsier, Nicolaas.

"Heer, Engel, Borges." (In: *New Found Land*, Jaargang I, no. 1, p. 41. Amsterdam, September 1981).

815. Maxence, Michel.

"Meriter Borges." (In: *Cahiers de L'Herne*, no. 4, pp. [1-3]. Paris, 1964).

Article appears as "Avant-propos" to this issue. 3 copies.

816. Mc Murray, George R.

Jorge Luis Borges. New York: Frederick Ungar Publishing Co., [1980].
[i-vi] vii-xxvii, 1-255 [256-258] p. 20.5 cm.
(Modern literature monographs.)

817. Meijsing, Doeschka.

[Untitled article on Borges' poem "El ángel."]
(In: *New Found Land,* Jaargang I, no. 1, pp. 42-43. Amsterdam, September 1981).

818. Melendes, Joserramón.

En Borges. [Riopiedras, Puerto Rico: QeAse, 1980].
[1-8] 9-139 [140-144] p. 20.5 cm.

First edition.

819. Milleret, Jean de.

"Biographie." (In: *Cahiers de L'Herne,* no. 4, pp. 476-479. Paris, 1964).

Borges chronology. 3 copies.

BECCO 943

820. Miniére, Claude.

"Non, il n'est pas certain que Dieu seul suffise." (In: *Europe,* no. 637, pp. [50]-52. Paris, May 1982).

821. Molachino, Justo R.

En torno a Borges. Justo R. Molachino. Jorge Mejía Prieto. [Buenos Aires:] Hachette, [1984].

[1-5] 6-191 [192] p. 21 cm.

2 copies.

822. Molloy, Silvia.

"Borges y la distancia literaria." (In: *Sur*, no. 318, pp. [26]-37. Buenos Aires, May-June 1969).

BECCO 951

823. Molloy, Silvia.

"Isidro Parodi: varios problemas para el traductor." (In: *Sur*, no. 312, pp. [71]-74. Buenos Aires, May-June 1968).

BECCO 950

824. Molloy, Silvia.

Las letras de Borges. Buenos Aires: Editorial Sudamericana, [1979].
[1-9] 10-220 [221-228] p. 19.5 cm.

825. Molloy, Silvia.

"Les lettres de Borges." (In: *Europe*, no. 637, pp. [93]-102. Paris, May 1982).

826. Montalbán, Juan.

"Glossaire argentin." (In: *Cahiers de L'Herne*, no. 4, pp. 480-484. Paris, 1964).

3 copies.

827. Montecchia, M. P.

Reportaje a Borges. Buenos Aires: Ediciones Crisol, [1977].
[1-6] 7-123 [124-128] p. 19.5 cm.

828. Mosca, Stefania.

Jorge Luis Borges: Utopia y realidad. [Caracas:] Monte Avila Editores, C.A., [1983].
[1-12] 13-157 [158-160] p. 17.5 cm.
(Colección estudios.)

829. Mourey, Jean-Pierre.

"L'échaiquier de Borges." (In: *Europe*, no. 637, pp. [34]-39. Paris, May 1982).

830. Mújica Laínez, Manuel.

"Borges et les ancêtres." (In: *Cahiers de L'Herne*, no. 4, pp. 151-155. Paris, 1964).

Appears in "Situation" section. 3 copies.

BECCO 967

831. Murillo, Luis Andrés.

"El immortal." (In: *Cahiers de L'Herne*, no. 4, pp. 293-308. Paris, 1964).

Appears in "Essais" section. 3 copies.

BECCO 974

832. Nadeau, Maurice.

"Borges la perturbateur." (In: *Cahiers de L'Herne*, no. 4, pp. 109-110. Paris, 1964).

Appears in "Interférences" section. 3 copies.

BECCO 997

833. Nagel, Ola Eggenschwiler.

"La noche y la muerte en el universo fantástico de Borges y de Beuzzati." (In: *Inti*, no. 9, pp. 65-78. Providence, Spring 1979).

834. Nalé Roxlo, Conrado.

Antología apócrifa. Caricaturas de Toño Salazar. [Buenos Aires:] Emecé, [1952].
[1-8] 9-234 [235-236] p. 20.5 cm.
(Sección Emecé de obras contemporáneas.)

Includes title: "A la manera de Jorge Luis Borges: 'Homicidio filosófico'." 2 copies.

835. Ocampo, Silvina.

"Images de Borges." (In: *Cahiers de L'Herne*, no. 4, pp. 26-30. Paris, 1964).

Appears in "Des témoins" section. 3 copies.

BECCO 992

836. Ocampo, Silvina.

"El pensamiento: a Borges." (In: *Clarín: cultura y nación*, p. 3. Buenos Aires, 23 August 1979).

Gift of C. Jared Loewenstein.

837. Ocampo, Victoria.

"Carta a Jorge Luis Borges." (In: *Cuadernos*, no. 88, pp. 41-42. Paris, September 1964).

838. Ocampo, Victoria.

"Norah Borges on Her Brother: An Unpublished Interview." (In: *Tri Quarterly*, no. 25, pp. 441-443. Evanston, Ill., Fall 1972).

Translated from Spanish.

839. Ocampo, Victoria.

"Visión de Jorge Luis Borges." (In: *Cuadernos*, no. 55, pp. 17-23. Paris, December 1961).

2 copies.

BECCO 994

840. Ocampo, Victoria.

"Visions de Jorge Luis Borges." (In: *Cahiers de L'Herne*, no. 4, pp. 19-25. Paris, 1964).

Appears in "Des témoins" section. 3 copies.

BECCO 995

841. *Ocho escritores: Martínez Estrada, Marechal, Borges, Bioy Casares, Quiroga, Groussac, Lugones, Macedonio Fernández. Por ocho periodistas: Avellaneda, Baracchini, Mahieu, Rivera, Couselo, Páez de la Torre, Casasbellas, Troiani.* [Buenos Aires:] Timerman Editores, [1976].
[1-6] 7-127 [128] p. 19.5 cm.

842. O'Hara, J. D.

"Richard Burgin: *Conversations with Jorge Luis Borges.*" (In: *Review '69*, pp. 66-68. New York, 1970).

843. Ollier, Claude.

"Thème du texte et du complot." (In: *Cahiers de L'Herne*, no. 4, pp. 276-279. Paris, 1964).

Appears in "Essais" section. 3 copies.

BECCO 1004

844. Orce Remis, Guillermo.

Seis destinos y otros rostros. Buenos Aires: Ediciones Troquel, [1963].
[1-8] 9-102 [103-104] p. 20 cm.
(Colección diálogos del presente, 15.)

BECCO 1008

845. Osorio G., Jairo.

Borges: memoria de un gesto. Jairo Osorio G. Carlos Bueno O. [Medellín: Ediciones Hombre Nuevo, 1979].
[i-ii], [1-10] 11-68 [69-70] p. 21 cm.

846. Paoli, Roberto.

Borges. Percorsi di significato. Messina-Firenze: Casa Editrice D'Anna, [1977].
[1-9] 10-162 [163-164] p. 21 cm.
(Universitá degli Studi di Firenze. Facoltá di Magistero. Istituto Ispanico. Publicazioni.)

847. Paseyro, Ricardo.

"Ce qui gêne ma vue." (In: *Cahiers de L'Herne*, no. 4, p. 117. Paris, 1964).

Appears in "Interférences" section. 3 copies.

BECCO 1026

848. Peltzer, Federico.

"Les masques de Borges." (In: *Cahiers de L'Herne*, no. 4, pp. 179-184. Paris, 1964).

Appears in "Situation" section. 3 copies.

BECCO 1030

849. Peralta, Carlos.

"L'électricité des mots." (In: *Cahiers de L'Herne*, no. 4, pp. 409-413. Paris, 1964).

Appears in "Entretiens avec" section. 3 copies.

BECCO 1032

850. Pereda Valdés, Ildefonso.

"Memorial de 'Martín Fierro'." (In: *Testigo*, no. 3, pp. 18-24. Buenos Aires, July-September 1966).

851. Pereira Lahitte, Carlos T. de.

"Généalogie de Jorge Luis Borges." (In: *Cahiers de L'Herne*, no. 4, pp. 156-158. Paris, 1964).

Appears in "Situation" section. 3 copies.

BECCO 1035

852. Petit de Murat, Ulyses.

Borges Buenos Aires. [Buenos Aires:] Municipalidad de la Ciudad de Buenos Aires. Secretaría de Cultura, [1980].
[1-14] 15-220 [221-224] p. 24.5 cm.

853. Pezzoni, Enrique.

"Aproximación al último libro de Borges." (In: *Sur*, no. 217-218, pp. [101]-123. Buenos Aires, November-December 1952).

Article appearing in "Crónica" section. Discussion of Borges' *Otras inquisiciones.* 2 copies.

BECCO 1046

854. Pickenhayn, Jorge Oscar.

Borges a través de sus libros. [Buenos Aires:] Plus Ultra, [1979].
[1-6] 7-252 [253-256] p. 20 cm.

855. Pickenhayn, Jorge Oscar.

Borges: álgebra y fuego. Vida y obra del gran escritor argentino. [Buenos Aires:] Editorial de Belgrano, [1982].
[1-9] 10-189 [190-192] p. 20 cm.
(Colección ensayos.)

856. Pinto, Juan.

Panorama de la literatura argentina contemporánea. Buenos Aires: Editorial Mundi, 1941.
[1-6] 7-385 [386-400] p. 20.5 cm.

Includes brief biography and critical discussion of Borges, pp. 53-56.

857. Pontes, José Couto.

Jorge Luis Borges, a erudição e os espelhos. [São Paulo: Vaner Bícego,] 1976.
[1-11] 12-53 [54-64] p. 21 cm.

858. "El premio a Borges." (In: *La vida literaria; crítica, información bibliográfica*, Año I, no. 11, p. 8. Buenos Aires, June 1929).

859. "Los premios nacionales de literatura." (In: *Nosotros*, Segunda Epoca, Año VII, no. 76, pp. 114-116. Buenos Aires, July 1942).

Discussion on p. 116 concerning Borges' *El jardín de senderos que se bifurcan.*

860. Prescott, Peter S.

"Jorge Luis Borges: *The Book of Imaginary Beings.*" (In: *Review '69*, pp. 52-54. New York, 1970).

861. Prieto, Adolfo.

"Borges, el ensayo crítico." (In: *Centro*, Año III, no. 7, pp. [9]-19. Buenos Aires, December 1953).

BECCO 1084

862. "Los primeros poemas de Borges." (In: *Testigo*, no. 3, pp. 109-110. Buenos Aires, July-September 1966).

Article appearing in "Crónica" section. Includes "Trinchera" and "Tranvías," two of Borges' earliest published verses.

863. Puente, Graciela Susana.

Borges, Molinari, Juarroz. Noche, sed, absurdo.
Dibujos de: Osvaldo Svanascini. [Buenos Aires:]
Botella al Mar, [1984].
[1-6] 7-65 [66-72] p. 20 cm.

864. Rabi.

"Fascination de la kabbale." (In: *Cahiers de L'Herne*, no. 4, pp. 265-271. Paris, 1964).

Appears in "Essais" section. 3 copies.

BECCO 1094

865. Ramírez Molas, Pedro.

Tiempo y narración. Enfoques de la temporalidad en Borges, Carpentier, Cortázar, y García Márquez.
Madrid: Editorial Gredos, [1978].
[1-9] 10-217 [218-236] p. 19.5 cm.
(Biblioteca románica hispánica, II. Estudios y ensayos, 276.)

2 copies.

866. Ramos, Jorge Abelardo.

Crisis y resurrección de la literatura argentina.
Apéndice: Polémica Sábato-Ramos. Buenos Aires:
Ediciones Coyoacán, 1961.
[1-8] 9-78 [79-80] p. 18 cm.
(Ediciones Coyoacan, 17.)

Second edition.

BECCO 1100

867. Rasi, Humberto M.

"The Final Creole: Borges' View of Argentine History." (In: *Tri Quarterly*, no. 25, pp. 149-171. Evanston, Ill., Fall 1972).

868. Regalado, Antonio, Jr.

"Le refus de l'histoire." (In: *Cahiers de L'Herne*, no. 4, pp. 352-361. Paris, 1964).

Appears in "Essais" section. 3 copies.

BECCO 1105

869. Reid, Alastair.

"Borges as Reader." (In: *Tri Quarterly*, no. 25, pp. 100-101. Evanston, Ill., Fall 1972).

870. Rest, Jaime.

El laberinto del universo: Borges y el pensamiento nominalista. Buenos Aires: Ediciones Librerías Fausto, [1976].
[1-11] 12-201 [202-208] p. 19.5 cm.
(Textos de apoyo.)

First edition. 2 copies.

871. Revol, E[nrique] L[uis].

La tradición imaginada, de Joyce a Borges. Córdoba: [Taller Editor de la Universidad Nacional de Córdoba,] 1971.
[1-6] 7-156 [157-160] p. 23 cm.

Essays, some previously published in various newspapers and periodicals. Includes bibliographical references. 2 copies.

BECCO 1111

872. Reyes, Alfonso.

"L'Argentin Jorge Luis Borges." (In: *Cahiers de L'Herne*, no. 4, pp. 103-104. Paris, 1964).

Appears in "Interférences" section. 3 copies.

BECCO 1116

873. Ricardou, Jean.

"The God of the Labyrinth." (In: *Cahiers de L'Herne*, no. 4, pp. 125-126. Paris, 1964).

Appears in "Interférences" section. 3 copies.

BECCO 1120

874. "Richard Burgin: *Conversations with Jorge Luis Borges*." (In: *Review '69*, p. 66. New York, 1970).

Originally published in *The New Yorker*, 12 July 1969.

875. Ríos, Julián.

"Mots croises." (In: *Europe*, no. 637, pp. [115]-119. Paris, May 1982).

876. Ríos Patrón, José Luis.

Jorge Luis Borges. Buenos Aires: Editorial "La Mandrágora," [1955].
[1-9] 10-179 [180] p. 17.5 cm.
(Clásicos argentinos del siglo XX.)

BECCO 1126

877. Ríos Patrón, José Luis.

"El laberinto de Borges." (In: *Sur*, no. 233, pp. 75-79. Buenos Aires, March-April 1955).

BECCO 1124

2 copies.

878. Risso Platero, Ema.

"En marchant près de Borges." (In: *Cahiers de L'Herne*, no. 4, pp. 31-32. Paris, 1964).

Appears in "Des témoins" section. 3 copies.

BECCO 1127

879. Rivas, José Andrés.

Alrededor de la obra de Jorge Luis Borges. Santiago del Estero, Argentina: Dirección General de Cultura de la Provincia, 1980.
[i-viii], [1-8] 9-156 [157-158] p. 18.5 cm.

880. Rodman, Selden.

"Richard Burgin: *Conversations with Jorge Luis Borges*." (In: *Review '69*, pp. 68-72. New York, 1970).

881. Rodríguez Monegal, Emir.

"Borges essayiste." (In: *Cahiers de L'Herne*, no. 4, pp. 343-351. Paris, 1964).

Appears in "Essais" section. 3 copies.

882. Rodríguez Monegal, Emir.

Borges, hacia una lectura poética. Madrid: Ediciones Guadarrama, 1976.
[1-6] 7-127 [128] p. 18.5 cm.
(Ediciones de bolsillo; 478: literatura.)

Includes bibliographical references. Cover title: *Borges: hacia una interpretación.* 2 copies.

883. Rodríguez Monegal, Emir.

Borgès par lui-meme. Traduction Françoise-Marie Rosset. [Paris:] Editions du Seuil, 1970.
[1-4] 5-188 [189-192] p. 18 cm.
("Ecrivains de toujours," 86.)

BECCO 1150

884. Rodríguez Monegal, Emir.

Borges por él mismo. Barcelona: Editorial Laia, [1983].
[i-ii], [1-6] 7-255 [256-258] p. 20 cm.
(Laia/ literatura.)

First edition.

885. Rodríguez Monegal, Emir.

"Borges: The Reader as Writer." (In: *Tri Quarterly*, no. 25, pp. 102-143. Evanston, Ill., Fall 1972).

886. Rodríguez Monegal, Emir.

Borges: uma poética da leitura. [São Paulo:] Editora Perspectiva, [1980].
[1-6] 7-187 [188] p. 20.5 cm.

887. Rodríguez Monegal, Emir.

Jorge Luis Borges: A Literary Biography. New York: E. P. Dutton, [1978].
[i-vii] viii-ix [x], [1-2] 3-502 p. 24 cm.

The definitive biographical study of Borges.

888. Rodríguez Monegal, Emir.

El juicio de los parricidas. La nueva generación argentina y sus maestros. Buenos Aires: Editorial Deucalión, [1956].
[1-6] 7-108 [109-112] p. 20 cm.
(Colección ahora y aquí, 2.)

Includes chapter "Borges entre Escila y Caribdis."

BECCO 1141

889. Rodríguez Monegal, Emir.

Mario de Andrade/ Borges. Um diálogo dos anos 20. [São Paulo: Editora Perspectiva, 1978].
[1-6] 7-126 [127-128] p. 15.5 cm.
(Coleção elos, 27.)

890. Rodríguez Monegal, Emir.

"The New Latin American Literature in USA." (In: *Review '68*, pp. 3-13. New York, 1969).

[BECCO 1115]

891. Rojas-Nix, Miguel.

"Borges, l'epée glorieuse et la dynamite furtive." (In: *Europe*, no. 637, pp. [14]-23. Paris, May 1982).

892. Running, Thorpe.

Borges' Ultraist Movement and Its Poets. Lathrup Village, Mich.: International Book Publishers, [1981].
[i-vi] vii-ix [x], 1-194 [195-198] p. 21.5 cm.
(Studies in language and literature.)

893. Sabat, Hermenegildo.

Georgie dear. [Buenos Aires: Editorial Crisis, 1974.]

24 unnumbered leaves [pp. 1-48]. 21 cm.

894. Sábato, Ernesto.

Claves políticas. [Buenos Aires:] Rodolfo Alonso Editor, [1972].
[1-9] 10-122 [123-128] p. 18 cm.
(Colección documentos.)

Second edition.

BECCO 1187

895. Sábato, Ernesto.

"Les deux Borges." (In: *Cahiers de L'Herne,* no. 4, pp. 168-178. Paris, 1964).

Appears in "Situation" section. 3 copies.

BECCO 1182

896. Sábato, Ernesto.

"Una efusión de Jorge Luis Borges." (In: *Ficción,* no. 4, pp. [80]-82. Buenos Aires, November-December 1956).

BECCO 1177

897. Sábato, Ernesto.

"Sobre el método histórico de Jorge Luis Borges." (In: *Ficción*, no. 7, pp. [86]-89. Buenos Aires, May-June 1957).

BECCO 1178

898. Sábato, Ernesto.

Tres aproximaciones a la literatura de nuestro tiempo: Robbe-Grillet, Borges, Sartre. [Santiago:] Editorial Universitaria, S.A., [1968].
[1-11] 12-93 [94-96] p. 18 cm.
(Colección letras de América, 12.)

BECCO 1185

899. Salvador, Nélida.

Revistas argentinas de vanguardia (1920-1930). [Buenos Aires:] Universidad de Buenos Aires. Facultad de Filosofía y Letras, [1962].
[1-8] 9-108 [109-112] p. 19 cm.
(Instituto de Literatura Argentina "Ricardo Rojas.")

Discussion of various Argentine literary magazines of the period cited, including a number founded by Borges or containing his contributions.

900. Salvador, Nélida.

"Las revistas de una época literaria: 'Florida-Boedo'." (In: *Testigo*, no. 3, pp. 40-44. Buenos Aires, July-September 1966).

901. Sánchez, Luis Alberto.

Historia de la literatura americana (Desde los orígenes hasta 1936). Santiago: Ediciones Ercilla, 1937.
[1-9] 10-681 [682-684] p. 18 cm.

Gift of Raul d'Eça.

902. Schallman, Lázaro.

Coloquios sobre el lenguaje argentino. Prólogo Juan B. Selva. Buenos Aires: Librería y Editorial El Ateneo, 1946.
[1-5] 6-291 [292-296] p. 24 cm.

Numerous references to Borges in text.

903. Schneider, Luis Mario.

"La place de Borges dans une histoire du langage argentin." (In: *Cahiers de L'Herne*, no. 4, pp. 137-143. Paris, 1964).

Appears in "Situation" section. 3 copies.

BECCO 1205

904. Shaw, Donald L.

Ficciones: Jorge Luis Borges. Barcelona: Editorial Laia, 1986.
[1-5] 6-135 [136] p. 19 cm.
(Guías Laia de literatura, 11.)

2 copies.

905. Silva, Mario Camarinha da.

Destino e concentração. (Uma teoria da arte de Jorge Luis Borges). Tese de concurso para provimento da cadeira de Literaturas Hispano-Americanas da Faculdade Nacional de Filosofia da Universidade do Brasil. Rio de Janeiro: [Universidade do Brasil,] 1957.
[1-4] 5-112 [113-114] p. (recto only) 28.5 cm.

906. Simon, John.

"Jorge Luis Borges: *A Personal Anthology*." (In: *Review '68*, pp. 43-47. New York, 1969).

907. Simon, John.

"Jorge Luis Borges: *The Book of Imaginary Beings*." (In: *Review '69*, pp. 54-57. New York, 1970).

908. *Simply a Man of Letters. Panel Discussions and Papers from the Proceedings of a Symposium on Jorge Luis Borges Held at the University of Maine at Orono*. Orono: University of Maine at Orono Press, 1982.
[i-iii] iv-ix [x], [1] 2-353 [354-362] p. 23.5 cm.

Papers edited by Carlos Cortínez.

909. Sosnowski, Saúl.

Borges y la cábala: la búsqueda del verbo. Buenos Aires: Ediciones Hispamérica, [1976].
[1-12] 13-119 [120] p. 18 cm.

First edition. 2 copies.

910. Sosnowski, Saúl.

"Jorge Luis Borges." (In: *Hispamérica*, Año III, no. 8, pp. [55]-60. Buenos Aires, October 1974).

Article appearing in "Entrevistas" section.

911. Stabb, Martin S.

Jorge Luis Borges. [New York:] Twayne Publishers, [1970].
[1-12] 13-179 [180-184] p. 21 cm.

(Twayne's World Authors Series. TWAS 108. Argentina.)

BECCO 1228

912. Sturrock, John.

Paper Tigers: The Ideal Fictions of Jorge Luis Borges. Oxford: Clarendon Press, 1977.
[i-x], [1] 2-277 [228] p. 22 cm.

913. Sucre, Guillermo.

"La biografía del infinito." (In: *Eco,* no. 125, pp. [466]-502. Bogotá, September 1970).

BECCO 1237

914. Sucre, Guillermo.

Borges, el poeta. México: Universidad Nacional Autónoma de México, 1967.
[i-ii], [1-8] 9-125 [126-130] p. 19.5 cm.
(Colección poemas y ensayos.)

First edition.

BECCO 1234

915. Sucre, Guillermo.

Borges, el poeta. Ensayo. [Caracas:] Monte Avila Editores, [1974, c. 1967].
[1-8] 9-157 [158-160] p. 18 cm.
(Colección letra viva.)

Second edition. 4 copies.

[BECCO 1234]

916. Tamayo, Marcial.

Borges, enigma y clave. Marcial Tamayo. Adolfo Ruiz-Díaz. Buenos Aires: Editorial Nuestro Tiempo, [1955].
[1-8] 9-170 [171-176] p. 20.5 cm.

2 copies.

BECCO 1244

917. Tealdi, Juan Carlos.

Borges y Viñas. (Literatura e ideología). [Madrid:] Editorial Orígenes, [1983].
[1-16] 17-168 [169-176] p. 20 cm.
(Colección tratados de crítica literaria.)

918. Theroux, Alexander.

"Jorge Luis Borges." (In: *Andover Bulletin*, Vol. 77, no. 1, pp. 6-7. Andover, Summer 1983).

Gift of Evan Bonds.

919. Theroux, Paul.

The Old Patagonian Express: By Train through the Americas. Boston: Houghton Mifflin Company, 1979.
[i-xii], [1] 2-404 p. 23.5 cm.

Includes a chapter on Borges entitled "The Buenos Aires Subterranean."

920. "Todo Borges y . . . " (In: *Libro elegido*, no. 5, pp. 140-151. Buenos Aires, August-September 1976).

Review of title published by Editorial Atlántida.

921. *Todo Borges y . . .* [Buenos Aires: Editorial Atlántida, 1977].
[1-3] 4-209 [210-212] p. 32 cm.
(Gente y la actualidad.)

2 copies.

922. Torre, Guillermo de.

"Pour la préhistoire ultraiste de Borges." (In: *Cahiers de L'Herne*, no. 4, pp. 159-167. Paris, 1964).

Appears in "Situation" section. Article followed by 5 of Borges' earliest poems in French translation. 3 copies.

BECCO 1257

923. Vax, Louis.

Arte y literatura fantásticas. [Buenos Aires:] Editorial Universitaria de Buenos Aires, [1965].
[1-4] 5-127 [128] p. 18 cm.
(Lectores de Eudeba, 80.)

Translation of: *L'art et la littérature fantastiques.*

[BECCO 1273]

924. Vax, Louis.

"Borges philosophe." (In: *Cahiers de L'Herne*, no. 4, pp. 252-256. Paris, 1964).

Appears in "Essais" section. 3 copies.

BECCO 1274

925. Vázquez, María Esther.

Borges: imágenes, memorias, diálogos. [Caracas:] Monte Avila Editores. S.A., [1977].

[1-10] 11-240 [241-248] p. 17.5 cm.
(Colección estudios.)

2 copies.

926. Vázquez, María Esther.

Colloqui con Borges. Immagini, memorie, visioni. Prefazione di Jorge Luis Borges. [Palermo:] Novecento, [1982].
[1-6] 7-374 [375-376] p. 20 cm.
(Narciso di novecento, 3.)

Italian translation of: *Borges: imágenes, memorias, diálogos.* First edition.

927. Vázquez, María Esther.

Everness (un ensayo sobre Jorge Luis Borges). [Buenos Aires:] Falbo Librero, Editor, [1965].
[1-8] 9-21 [22-24] p. 17.5 cm.

2 copies.

BECCO 1275

928. Vázquez, María Esther.

"L'homme Borges." (In: *Europe*, no. 637, pp. [40]-49. Paris, May 1982).

929. Vázquez, Nélida E.

Borges: la humillación de ser hombre. [Buenos Aires:] Febra Editores, [1981].
[i-ii], [1-4] 5-85 [86-88] p. 18.5 cm.

2 copies.

930. Vian, Cesco.

Invito alla lettura di Jorge Luis Borges. [Milano:] Mursia, [1980].
[1-5] 6-222 [223-224] p. 17 cm.
(Invito alla lettura. Sezione straniera, 28/29.)

931. Videla, Gloria.

"Poemas y prosas olvidadas de Borges." (In: *Revista de literatura argentina e iberoamericana,* no. 3, pp. [101]-105. Mendoza, Argentina, December 1961).

Includes portions of Borges' earliest poetic texts, notably the famous "Himno del mar."

BECCO 1285

932. Videla, Gloria.

"Presencia americana en el ultraísmo español." (In: *Revista de literatura argentina e iberoamericana,* no. 3, pp. [7]-25. Mendoza, Argentina, December 1961).

Discussion of Borges appears on pp. 20-25.

BECCO 1284

933. *Vierunddreissig neue Kurzgeschichten aus der Zeit.* Herausgegeben von Dieter E. Zimmer. [Hamburg:] Hoffman und Campe, [1979].
[1-6] 7-324 [325-328] p. 20.5 cm.

934. Villarino, María de.

"Las llaves, Borges." (In: *Letras de Buenos Aires,* Año I, no. 1, pp. 45-46. Buenos Aires, October-December 1980).

935. Villordo, Oscar Hermes.

"El tercer Borges." (In: *Lyra: Argentina en positivo*, Año XXXVI, no. 237/9, pp. 36-37. Buenos Aires, 1978).

Gift of C. Jared Loewenstein.

936. Wahl, Jean.

"Les personnes et l'impersonal." (In: *Cahiers de L'Herne*, no. 4, pp. 257-264. Paris, 1964).

Appears in "Essais" section. 3 copies.

BECCO 1294

937. Wapuir, Salomón.

A izquierda y derecha. Semblanzas y contornos literarios. Buenos Aires: M. Gleizer--Editor, 1931.
[1-7] 8-171 [172-176] p. 19 cm.

Mentions Borges' early writings. Inscribed by the author: "Al amigo/Carlos Acquarone,/recuerdo de unos días/por tierras de provincia,/en lucha por el vil/ sustento . . . /con el afecto de/Wapuir/Junin--21-3-34--."

938. Wapuir, Salomón.

Hombres y paisajes de la Argentina. Buenos Aires: Editorial Claridad, [1966].
[1-9] 10-199 [200] p. 20.5 cm.
(Colección arco iris, 12.)

First edition. Brief mention of Borges and his poetry.

939. Wheelock, Carter.

"Borges' New Prose." (In: *Tri Quarterly*, no. 25, pp. 403-440. Evanston, Ill., Fall 1972).

940. Wolberg, Isaac.

Jorge Luis Borges. [Buenos Aires:] Ediciones Culturales Argentinas. Ministerio de Educación y Justicia. Dirección General de Cultura, [1961].
[1-6] 7-84 [85-88] p. 25 cm.
(Biblioteca del sesquicentenario. Serie argentinos en las letras.)

Includes frontispiece portrait of Borges and four additional unnumbered leaves of illustrations in text.
2 copies.

BECCO 1303

941. Wright, John.

"Borges and Hawthorne." (In: *Tri Quarterly*, no. 25, pp. 334-355. Evanston, Ill., Fall 1972).

942. Yurkievich, Saül.

"Borges, poète circulaire." (In: *Europe*, no. 637, pp. [53]-65. Paris, May 1982).

943. Zuleta, Emilia de.

Relaciones literarias entre España y la Argentina. Madrid: Ediciones Cultura Hispánica del Instituto de Cooperación Iberoamericana, 1983.
[1-6] 7-278 [279-280] p. 22 cm.

XII. INTERVIEWS

944. Alcorta, Gloria.

"Entretiens avec Gloria Alcorta." (In: *Cahiers de L'Herne*, no. 4, pp. 404-408. Paris, 1964).

Interview between Alcorta and Borges. Appears in "Entretiens avec" section. 3 copies.

BECCO 333

945. Alifano, Roberto.

Conversando con Borges. [Buenos Aires: Siete Días Ilustrados, 1981].
[1-2] 3-31 [32] p. 26 cm.
(Cuadernos de Siete Días.)

Supplement to the magazine *Siete Días*, no. 748.

946. *Borges at Eighty. Conversations*. Edited and with photographs by Willis Barnstone. Bloomington: Indiana University Press, [1982].
[i-vii] viii-xii [xiii-xiv], 1-176 [177-178] p. 24 cm.

947. "Borges at N.Y.U." (In: *Tri Quarterly*, no. 25, pp. 444-459. Evanston, Ill., Fall 1972).

Text of Borges' remarks before a group of students at New York University. Alexander Coleman moderated the session, held on 8 April 1971. Ronald Christ edited the version that appears here.

948. *Borges el memorioso*. Conversaciones de Jorge Luis Borges con Antonio Carizo. México-Buenos Aires: Fondo de Cultura Económica, [1982].
[1-8] 9-313 [314-320] p. 23 cm.
(Colección tierra firme.)

949. *Borges el memorioso.* Conversaciones de Jorge Luis Borges con Antonio Carrizo. México: Fondo de Cultura Económica, [1983, c. 1982].
[1-8] 9-313 [314-320] p. 23 cm.
(Colección tierra firme.)

Second edition.

2 copies.

950. Burgin, Richard.

Conversaciones con Jorge Luis Borges. Versión española de Manuel R. Coronado, revisada por Roberto Yahni. [Madrid:] Taurus, [1974].
[1-12] 13-161 [162-164] p. 21 cm.
(Persiles, 70).

Original title: *Conversations with Jorge Luis Borges.* 2 copies.

[BECCO 506]

951. Burgin, Richard.

Conversations with Jorge Luis Borges. New York, Chicago, San Francisco: Holt, Rinehart and Winston, [1969].
[i-iv] v-xvi, 1-144 p. 21.5 cm.

Gift of Joan St. C. Crane.

BECCO 506

952. Campra, Rosalba.

America Latina: L'identità e la maschera. Con interviste a Borges, Bosch, Carpentier, Cortázar, Galeano, Sábato, Scorza, Viñas, Walsh. [Rome:] Editori Riuniti, [1982].
[1-9] 10-226 [227-228] p. 19.5 cm.
(Universale, 63.) (Scienze sociali.)

First edition. Includes two interviews with Borges, pp. [115]-124.

953. Charbonnier, Georges.

El escritor y su obra. Entrevistas de Georges Charbonnier con Jorge Luis Borges. Traducción de Martí Soler. [México:] Siglo Veintiuno Editores, S.A., [1967].
[i-vi] vii [viii], 1-92 [93-96] p. 13 cm.
(Colección mínima literaria, 7.)

Translation of *Entretiens avec Jorge Luis Borges.* First edition in Spanish. 2 copies.

BECCO 590

954. Charbonnier, Georges.

El escritor y su obra. Entrevistas de Georges Charbonnier con Jorge Luis Borges. Traducción de Martí Soler. México: Siglo Veintiuno Editores, [1975].
[1-4] 5-97 [98-100] p. 15 cm.
(Colección mínima, 7.)

Third edition in Spanish.

[BECCO 590]

955. Childress, Mark.

"In the Looking Glass: An Interview with Jorge Luis Borges." (In: *Tulanian,* Vol. 53, no. 1, pp. 44-47. New Orleans, Spring 1982).

Joint author: Charles C. McNair. Includes reprint of "Borges and Myself" on p. 46. Gift of Aileen Ajootian.

956. Christ, Ronald J.

"Entrevista con Jorge Luis Borges." (In: *Facetas*, Vol. 3, no. 1, pp. 104-120. Washington, D.C., 1970).

BECCO 594

957. *Conversations avec J. L. Borges à l'occasion de son 80 anniversaire*. Présentées par Willis Barnstone. Traduites de l'américain par Anne Laflaquière. Paris: Editions Ramsay, [1984].
[1-7] 8-190 [191-198] p. 24 cm.

French translation of: *Borges at Eighty: Conversations.*

958. Elsass, Peter.

Emigrantliv. Kolonier, ghettoer-og folk pi flugt i Latinamerika. [Copenhagen:] Gyldendal, [1980].
[1-4] 5-285 [286-288] p. 22 cm.

Interview with Borges, pp. 92-109.

959. *Encuentro con Borges*. James Irby. Napoleón Murat. Carlos Peralta. [Buenos Aires:] Editorial Galerna, [1968].
[1-6] 7-112 [113-116] p. 18 cm.
(Colección testimonios.)

BECCO 819

960. *Encuesta a la literatura argentina contemporánea*. [Buenos Aires:] Centro Editor de América Latina, [1982].
[i-viii], 1-504 [505-512] p. 25.5 cm.

Interview with Borges by Noemí Ulla, pp. 217-226.

961. "Entrevue avec les élèves de Borges." (In: *Cahiers de L'Herne*, no. 4, pp. 48-52. Paris, 1964).

Appears in "Des témoins" section. 3 copies.

962. *Espejo de escritores. Entrevistas con Borges, Cortázar, Fuentes, Goytisolo, Onetti, Puig, Rama, Rulfo, Sánchez, Vargas Llosa.* Notas y prólogo de: Reina Roffé. [Hanover, N.H.:] Ediciones del Norte, [1985].
[i-vi] vii-xvi, [1] 2-222 [223-224] p. 20 cm.
(Espejo de escritores, 504.)

963. Grondona, Adela.

¿Por qué escribimos? Buenos Aires-Barcelona: Emecé Editores, [1969].
[1-10] 11-239 [240] p. 20 cm.
(Selección Emecé de obras contemporáneas.)

Interviews with various writers, some given as radio broadcasts, and some published previously in the periodical *Ficción*.

BECCO 761

964. Irby, James E.

"Entretiens avec James E. Irby." (In: *Cahiers de L'Herne*, no. 4, pp. 388-403. Paris, 1964).

Interview between Irby and Borges. Appears in "Entretiens avec" section. 3 copies.

BECCO 816

965. Leonardo, Sergio.

"Prefiero ser amado que admirado." (In: *Clarín: cultura y nación*, p. 2. Buenos Aires, 23 August 1979).

Gift of C. Jared Loewenstein.

966. Milleret, Jean de.

Entretiens avec Jorge Luis Borges. Paris: Editions Pierre Belfond, [1967].
[1-8] 9-255 [256] p. 18 cm.
(Collection “entretiens”.)

BECCO 944

967. Milleret, Jean de.

Entrevistas con Jorge Luis Borges. [Caracas:] Monte Avila Editores C.A., [1971, c. 1970].
[1-8] 9-186 [187-192] p. 19.5 cm.
(Colección prisma.)

Translation of *Entretiens avec Jorge Luis Borges,* by Gabriel Rodríguez. 2 copies.

BECCO 945

968. Murat, Napoléon.

“Entretiens avec Napoléon Murat.” (In: *Cahiers de L'Herne,* no. 4, pp. 371-387. Paris, 1964).

Interview between Murat and Borges. Appears in “Entretiens avec” section. 3 copies.

BECCO 969

969. Ocampo, Victoria.

Diálogo con Borges. Buenos Aires: Sur, [1969].
[1-6] 7-83 [84-88] p. 26 cm.

2 copies.

BECCO 998

970. Sorrentino, Fernando.

Seven Conversations with Jorge Luis Borges. Translation, additional notes, appendix of personalities mentioned by Borges, and translator's foreword by Clark M. Zlotchew. Troy, N.Y.: The Whitston Publishing Company, [1982].
[i-vii] viii-xvi, [1] 2-219 [220-224] p. 23.5 cm.

One of 700 copies.

971. Sorrentino, Fernando.

Siete conversaciones con Jorge Luis Borges. [Buenos Aires:] Casa Pardo, S.A., [1973].
[1-6] 7-161 [162-168] p. 20 cm.

First edition.

972. Stern, Richard.

The Invention of the Real. Athens: The University of Georgia Press, [1982].
[i-ix] x-xiii [xiv], [1] 2-233 [234] p. 22.5 cm.

Includes text of 1966 interview with Borges, entitled "Borges on Borges," pp. 27-45.

973. *Twenty-Four Conversations with Borges. Including a Selection of Poems. Interviews by Roberto Alifano 1981-1983.* Conversations translated by Nicomedes Suárez Araúz, Willis Barnstone and Noemí Escandell. Poems translated by Willis Barnstone, Jorge Luis Borges and Nicomedes Suárez Araúz. Photographs by Willis Barnstone. [Housatonic, Mass.:] Lascaux Publishers, [1984].
[i-viii] ix-xv [xvi], 1-157 [158-160] p. 23.5 cm. (Altamira Inter-American Series.)

974. Ventura, Any.

Sin anestesia. [Buenos Aires:] Editorial de Belgrano, [1982].
[1-7] 8-226 [227-232] p. 20 cm.
(Colección diálogos.)

Includes interview with Borges, pp. [43]-53.

XIII. BIBLIOGRAPHIES

975. Becco, Horacio Jorge.

Jorge Luis Borges. Bibliografía total, 1923-1973. Buenos Aires: Casa Pardo S.A., [1973]. [1-12] 13-244 [245-248] p. 26.5 cm.

The standard bibliography on Borges to date. Published to commemorate the fiftieth anniversary of Borges' first book, *Fervor de Buenos Aires.* 2 copies.

976. di Giovanni, Norman Thomas.

"Checklist of the Principal Works of Jorge Luis Borges." (In: *Tri Quarterly*, no. 25, pp. 463-465. Evanston, Ill., Fall 1972).

977. Foster, David William.

Jorge Luis Borges: An Annotated Primary and Secondary Bibliography. Introduction by Martin S. Stabb. New York/London: Garland Publishing, Inc., 1984.
[i-vi] vii-xlvi [xlvii-xlviii], 1-328 p. 22.5 cm.
(Garland Reference Library of the Humanities, 439.)

Most recent contribution to a comprehensive bibliography of Borges, with special emphasis upon critical works.

978. Lucio, Nodier.

"Contribución a la bibliografía de Jorge Luis Borges." (In: *Bibliografía argentina de artes y letras*, nos. 10-11, pp. [43]-112. Buenos Aires, April-September 1961).

Joint author: Lydia Revello. Published by the Fondo Nacional de las Artes. One of the earliest attempts at a comprehensive bibliography on Borges. 2 copies.

BECCO 1369

979. Lucio, Nodier.

"Contribution a la bibliographie de Borges." (In: *Cahiers de L'Herne*, no. 4, pp. [485]-516. Paris, 1964).

Joint author: Lydia Revello. 3 copies.

BECCO 1370

AUTHOR INDEX

TITLE INDEX

AUTHOR INDEX

References are to item numbers. Entries under "Jorge Luis Borges," excluding pseudonyms, are not indexed.

TITLE INDEX

References are to item numbers.